I0559176

KING

POWER HOUSE

KING

A Memoir

*Life Lessons Learned with the
Queen of My Heart*

Gene Paul King

Copyright © 2024 by Gene Paul King

All right reserved. This book is protected by the copyright laws of the United States of America. This book may not be copied or reprinted for commercial gain or profit. The use of short quotations or occasional page copying for personal study is permitted and encouraged, provided proper citation and credits are acknowledged. Permission will be granted upon request for appropriate usage.

Unless otherwise indicated, all Scripture quotations are from King James Version (KJV). Public Domain. Scripture quotations identified NKJV are taken from the New King James Version®. Copyright © 1982 by Thomas Nelson. Used by permission. All rights reserved.

Citations for sources, as well as supplemental information on historical events, churches, people, and places mentioned in the text, are included in the endnotes ("Notes").

Graphics and Interior Design by Dr. Michelle Everett for POWER HOUSE, © 2024 Power House Studios, LLC.

Published by: **Power House**

An imprint of Power House Studios LLC.

thepowerhousestudio.com

PO Box 101678

Cape Coral FL 33910

Home of *The Power House Blueprint*™ Concierge Publishing System

Dedication

I dedicate this book to my four children, Shannon Gene, Anthony Paul, Regena Renee, and Nathanael Paul.

And to our ten grandchildren: Misty "Paul" Ann, Clayton Gene, Rachel Alexandrea, Jordan Paul, Cody Franklin, Kathryn Marie, Hayden Chandler, Conner Avery "Paul," Gracie Marie, and Levi Henry; and our ten great-grandchildren (at the time this is published): Jacob, Blakely, Madison, Briggs, Riley, Lane, Zoe, Olivia, Evelyn, and Lainey Lynn.

Contents

Chapter One   1

Chapter Two   27

Chapter Three   41

Chapter Four   65

Chapter Five   83

Chapter Six   105

Chapter Seven   117

Chapter Eight   135

Epilogue   143

Thankful for Us (Additional Photos)   145

Appendix
    Notes   151

Meet the Author   161

Preface

It seems good in the preface to answer the obvious question, "Why would those outside of the immediate family want to read someone's memoir?"

KING is more than the memories of one man or even one family; it is a glimpse of humanity in all our struggles and successes. **KING** is **a piece of history** that includes records from many primary sources such as letters, newspaper articles, photographs, birth and death records, and first-hand accounts. Spanning decades of American Christian heritage, this book records relationships, events, and stories that comprise the history of several Assemblies of God churches, plus a few Baptist and non-denominational churches in Texas and Arkansas.

Amid family growth and great change, God worked all things together for the good of those who love Him and are called according to His purpose. You are invited to embark on a journey of discovery in this delightful, easy-to-read collection of life lessons learned with the queen of his heart, living for The King of kings (and The King of these Kings). We encourage you to laugh with the humorous accounts and antics along the way and reflect on how the Lord led, protected, and provided for this family-and still is!

What He has done for others, God will do for you.

Chapter One

It was at the early age of eight when I first felt the call of God on my life. Although I was young, I already knew the moving of the Holy Spirit, and I felt God tugging at my heart to preach the Gospel.

The King family was raised attending a historic Holiness church, which was started in the mid-1930s by Reverend Herbert A. Johnson. The church was just down from the house, on the corner of Blackjack Road and Main Street. The church was an independent church at that time, named Bethel Temple, and later became known as the Aubrey Assembly of God.

It was under his ministry that my mother and all three of her sisters were saved and baptized with the Holy

Ghost. To feel the prompting of the Holy Ghost was not strange in our family. However, in my mind, I didn't really want to become a holiness preacher because I had heard people downtown talking negatively about "those old holy rollers." At that age, I wanted to be liked by everyone, so I began to pull away and run from the call of God that I was feeling within my heart.

I got my start in this legacy of "holy rollers" on November 16, 1942. I was born at home to my parents, William Iley King[1] and Abbie Katherine (Wilson) King,[2] in Denton, Texas. I was delivered by a woman doctor named Dr. Pearce. When I was three years old, my parents moved the family to Aubrey, Texas (into that house just down from the church). In so many ways, for many generations, the family's move to Aubrey was of great significance. Over the years, the King family became woven into the history of the region, and Aubrey remains home to several of our generations.

The King family lived at the north end of town on a thirty-six-acre estate. We had no city water or sewerage in the north end of town. Dad and Uncle Leon O. Brockett[3] worked the railroad together, and together they hand-dug our well. We had an outhouse for a restroom. For those who may not know about that, an outhouse is a small outdoor building, often just a wooden shack, containing a wooden bench with a hole in the center (or, in nicer versions, there might be a toilet seat fastened to the bench) positioned over a hole in the ground, with no plumbing,

BABY GENE PAUL KING

GENE KING, CALLED TO PREACH AT
8 YEARS OLD

KING FAMILY MOVES TO AUBREY,
TX (AGE 3, RIGHT FRONT)

GENE KING'S DAD, ILEY KING (5TH FROM LEFT) AND UNCLE LEON
BROCKETT (4TH FROM LEFT), RAILROAD WORKERS IN THE 1940'S

3

GENE KING
FIRST GRADE

GENE KING
SECOND GRADE

GENE KING
THIRD GRADE

GENE KING
FOURTH GRADE

GENE KING
EIGHTH GRADE (DENTON)

GENE KING
ELEVENTH GRADE

and a variety of paper goods (magazines, catalogs, newspapers) or corn cobs might be used instead of toilet paper.

Our house and barn sat on the northwest corner of the property. Blackjack Road ran east and west on the north end of the property. A dirt lane (unnamed at the time but later named Brockett Street) ran north and south on the west side of the property. On the east side, old Highway 10 and the railroad tracks ran the entire length of the property. Willie Clyde Simpson (who once owned the pharmacy in Aubrey) and my father donated the land to open the east end of North Street to join old Highway 10 on the south end of the property.

As a kid growing up, I played and roamed the dirt streets of Aubrey. I had two older brothers, Monroe[4] and Jimmy[5], and one older sister, Lois[6]. Being the baby of the family for nine years, I was spoiled rotten, especially by my sister, who was ten years older than me. You might say this King was a little king for a time.

But then, much to my surprise, I suddenly had a baby brother. On July 9, 1951, baby Gaylon arrived in the family, and he promptly dethroned me! When mother brought baby brother home, neither our old bulldog nor I liked it one bit!

School Days

I started school in the first grade at Aubrey, and my teacher's name was Mrs. Tipps. I remember my first girlfriend in the first grade. Her desk was on the front row.

One day, I had gotten into trouble. The teacher made me bend over my girlfriend's desk, and the teacher paddled me until I cried in front of my girlfriend, who laughed at me. I think her laughing at me hurt my pride worse than the paddling hurt my backside!

My second-grade teacher was Mrs. Propper. I don't remember much about the second grade, except I thought my teacher was pretty! My third-grade teacher was Mrs. Miller. Mrs. Miller taught my sister Lois, who was ten years older than me, my brother Monroe, who was eight years older than me, and my brother Jimmy, who was four years older than me. So, I think Mrs. Miller must have been quite old when she taught me!

I believe my fourth-grade teacher's name was Mrs. Gamel, but I wasn't with her for very long. I had just started the fourth grade when our family sold the place in Aubrey and moved to Denton. I finished the fourth, fifth, and sixth grades at Jefferson Davis Elementary, and then I moved to Denton Junior High in the seventh grade.

When I was in the middle of the eighth grade, our family moved back near Aubrey to an old farmhouse in the middle of eighty acres, just two miles west of Aubrey, on West Blackjack Road.

The old farmhouse was built of boxing planks. The house had two big rooms, a kitchen, and a small enclosed back porch. There was no bathroom—actually, it had no indoor plumbing of any kind—so once again, our family of seven shared an outhouse as our only restroom!

I finished the eighth grade through the tenth grade at Aubrey. Since Aubrey School only went up to the tenth grade, high school students had to be bused to Pilot Point School for their junior and senior years of high school. I finished my junior year at Pilot Point, but I never went back for my senior year to graduate from Pilot Point High School.

I had so many adventures growing up in a small town without modern technology. I enjoyed every minute of my childhood, and do you know what? I survived! (But those are stories for a future book, so stay tuned for *a prequel*.)

Nancy's Early Years

It was almost springtime in Oklahoma, but a late winter storm had blanketed the ground with freezing snow and ice. Nevertheless, veteran (U.S. Army WWII) Edward Cranmore headed out in the wintry weather to fetch the doctor. His wife Marie was in labor in the small community of Antioch, Oklahoma. By the time he and the doctor arrived back at the house, my sweet Nancy had already made her appearance into this world.

In the year of our Lord 1949, on March 18, Nancy Ruth Cranmore was born to Edward Franklin Cranmore[7] and May Marie (Sons) Cranmore.[8] They lived in the rural area called Antioch, just off Highway 70, which ran between Madill and Ardmore, Oklahoma. The small rural community was located closer to Madill than to Ardmore. While waiting for the doctor to arrive, Nancy was born at home (I believe it was at her grandmother's house), delivered by her grandmother.

When Nancy was about seven years old, her family lived in the country just outside of Ardmore. Their house burned down, and they lost everything they owned in the fire. Sometime around the year 2015 or 2016, Nancy and our daughter took a girls' trip up to Oklahoma. Nancy found the spot where their house burned down, and a modern brick house was there now.

Nancy and Renee stopped and knocked on the door. When the man of the house answered the door, Nancy asked the man if she could get some dirt out of his yard (without any explanation). He looked at her, shocked, and went to get his wife. The wife came to the door right away to check on this crazy woman who was asking to get dirt from their yard! Nancy then explained the burning of their house when she was a little girl and the sentimental value a bit of the soil would have for her. When the man and woman realized that she wasn't some crazy person but understood why she wanted a little sample of dirt from that spot, the man grabbed a shovel. He gave her a container full of dirt to add to her collection of little jars of dirt from several places she played in while she was growing up.

Over the years, Nancy's dad mainly worked as a truck driver, hauling sand and rock for new road construction. The Cranmore family moved a lot while she was growing up. When Nancy was nine years old, the Cranmore family was in the process of moving from Oklahoma to

BABY NANCY (CRANMORE) KING

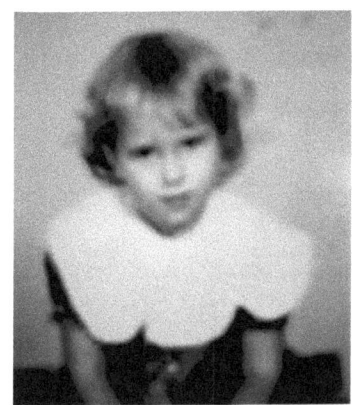

NANCY (CRANMORE) KING

NANCY (CRANMORE) KING
(ON LEFT)
WITH TWO OF HER SIBLINGS

9

NANCY (CRANMORE) KING
(IN THE MIDDLE OF
TWO OF HER SIBLINGS)

NANCY'S FAMILY
AS THEY MOVED TO AUBREY, TX

California. Along the way, the Cranmores stopped to visit relatives in Aubrey, Texas.

During their stay, Nancy caught a virus of some kind. She was sick for several days, which made it necessary for the family to extend their time in Aubrey. As a result, her dad decided he needed to get a job, and then, before they knew it, the Cranmore family had changed their moving plans and chosen to make Aubrey their home.

I do believe God had a hand in all of this. If they had not stopped over in town to stay with relatives, we might never have met! I believe God was preparing Nancy's heart to love and eventually meet and accept me into her life. Thus, the Mighty Hand of the Almighty was already at work to bring us together as a team to work together for His Kingdom.

The Cranmores bought a house on the west side of Aubrey. It was a four-room house with a front porch on a couple of acres of land. I mentioned earlier that her dad was a truck driver. Not only did her dad own and drive a truck, but he also would collect old junk cars to "junk out" (disassemble for parts to sell) during the worst days of winter. I remember that at one time, he had over a hundred old cars and trucks in the backyard at their house.

Mr. Cranmore also owned and operated a pool hall for a little while. And there was a short period of time when Nancy's dad owned and ran a Shell gas station downtown Aubrey. Mr. Cranmore liked to make a good profit and often traded or sold his cars and trucks if the deal was beneficial. In fact, he traded vehicles so often that he never fully filled his own gas tank up because Mr. Cranmore didn't want to give extra gas to whoever he might make a deal or trade with!

Nancy's mother had five sisters and two brothers. Four of the sisters lived near Nancy's former hometown of Ardmore. From those families, Nancy had several girl cousins, and the Cranmore family visited Ardmore often back then. (Fast forward a little bit here, but I had never been around such hugging people my whole life! Sad to say, I looked forward to the visits to Ardmore and thoroughly enjoyed the hugs.) Because of Mr. Cranmore's practice of not filling the cars up with gas in case he sold the vehicle, there was at least one time the Cranmore family started out to go to Ardmore, and before they were less than a mile out of Aubrey, they ran out of gas!

Beginning a Life (and unknowingly, a legacy)

After my school years, I worked in a grocery store for a while, and then I started a job in carpentry, which turned out to be the career that lasted most of my life. As time began to swiftly pass me by, I found myself unmarried at nearly twenty-one years old. Most of my friends my age were getting married right and left. A lot of my kinfolk were beginning to think I would end up an old bachelor.

I was nineteen and still running from the call of God. I had quit attending church and had drifted far from the peaceful shore. It was at this time in my life that I happened to see a particular young lady for the first time walking down the sidewalk on Main Street in Aubrey. I had no idea at that time that she would soon become the most important person in my life for the rest of my life.

She had walked to the post office and gotten her family's mail. Then, coming out of the Post Office, she began walking along reading a letter, all the while unknowingly dropping some of her pieces of mail. I stopped to pick up the pieces of mail that had fallen. Then I returned it to her and offered her a ride to her house. Not knowing me, of course, she refused to ride with me. So, I drove on down the road thinking, "Boy, oh boy! I'm going to get to know that beautiful young lady better someway, somehow!"

Several days later, without realizing it, I met Nancy's older sister, Carolyn,[9] at Joe and Audrey Stanley's cafe in Aubrey.[10] Now, I didn't know that she and Nancy were sisters, and I didn't know that Carolyn had already met and fallen in love with my cousin Kenneth Wilson.[11] So, I found out from someone where Carolyn lived and stopped by to ask her for a date.

I knocked on the door, but when Carolyn saw who was knocking, she wouldn't answer the door. Instead, and much to my surprise, she sent Nancy to answer the door. As the door opened, there, standing before me, was the most beautiful woman in the whole wide world!

This was my golden opportunity. Nancy remembered me from when I had picked up the fallen pieces of mail and offered her a ride home from the post office. We only talked through the screen door that day, but I was entirely sure that I wanted to speak with this beautiful girl again!

A few days later, I drove by Nancy's house to see what I could see. I saw her dad outside working on a car in their front yard. So, I seized the moment!

I stopped, introduced myself, and offered to help him as he was changing a motor from one car to another. Of course, I was really hoping to gain some brownie points with Nancy's dad that day! I reasoned that with a young lady of her caliber, I needed all the favor I could get. And it paid off!

I asked Nancy's father if I could take her to the drive-in picture show that night, and he said, "Yes if she is OK with it." Neither of us knew at the time that she already had plans to go with friends and be the date of another boy that night. However, persuaded by her father, Nancy did go with me to the drive-in that night, but not without a bit of theater (commotion) at the outdoor theater!

When we arrived at the drive-in, we discovered that the other boy whom she had first planned to go with had followed us there! After we parked, he circled our car several times. I guess he had the good sense not to challenge me over the matter and eventually moved on—perhaps he rightly guessed that I was 128 pounds of dynamite waiting to explode on him if he interfered with our first date! So, that's how our first date started off. Thankfully, before that night was over, I had won her heart over to love and hold forever and ever.

After Nancy found out that her sister's boyfriend and I were cousins, we often double-dated with them. We frequently had a party to go to, at least once a week, where we played games like "Spin the Bottle," "Thumbs Up and Thumbs Down," and "Name that Tune." Both of the couples continued to date, getting to know one another as we enjoyed bubble gum contests, hula-hoop contests, dancing, and having a good time together.

Popping the Big Question

Before Nancy and I married, I had rehearsed over and over how I was going to ask Mr. Cranmore if I could marry his daughter. I didn't want him to ever think I wasn't man enough to ask him for her hand in marriage. I knew Nancy, being as young as she was, must have either her dad or mother to sign for her to get married.

I was finally ready on one Sunday afternoon as I was riding in the car with her dad. I said, "Mr. Cranmore, can I marry your daughter?" His answer was, "Hell no." Well, that was not at all what I was expecting to hear! I sat silent for a while because, you see, I had never rehearsed what I'd say if he said no! So, what did I do? Dumb me, I just repeated the same question and my practiced lines. Mr. Cranmore answered again but added a whole lot more to his answer this time! Unfortunately, the answer was still the same. NO. After that exchange, he and I both rode in awkward silence the rest of the way to the Cranmore house.

On Sunday afternoons, it was common for some of the Ardmore kinfolks to be visiting. When Nancy's dad and I walked into their house, I quickly looked around at all who were gathered. Emboldened by their presence, I decided to bravely ask Nancy's dad the same question all over again in front of all the family and kinfolks in the room!

I could see that Mr. Cranmore was really getting mad, but by then, and in the courage of being surrounded by so many kinfolk, I didn't care. I was determined to marry my sweet Nancy. As Mr. Cranmore was stomping out of the room, he suddenly turned around and said, "If her mother wants to sign for Nancy to marry you, she'll have a son-in-law, and I will have one!" (Mr. Cranmore liked my cousin Kenneth, who had just married Nancy's sister Carolyn.) Determinedly, I spouted off that I'd accept that arrangement any day of the week!

You see, I didn't care if Mr. Cranmore liked me or not. I had already fallen in love not only with Nancy but also with her mother and her mother's cooking! But Nancy's mother had some questions of her own. Nancy's mother looked at her and asked Nancy if she *had* to get married. Quickly, before Nancy could say anything, I answered, "Yes!" Nancy slapped me real hard and replied to her mother, "No, Mother, it is not what you are thinking!" Nancy knew her mother was asking if Nancy was in a "family way" already! (That was a polite way of asking if Nancy was pregnant already.) That was not the case, but I had said yes because I was determined for us to get married one way or another. Thankfully, her mother stood with us and consented to sign for Nancy to be married.

The following day, Nancy, her mother, and I drove over to the Denton County Courthouse to get our marriage license. Back then, all the parking spaces around the courthouse had parking meters. I parked in one space and put my nickel in the parking meter next to the space where I had parked.

Once inside the courthouse, we filled out the necessary paperwork, and a court clerk, an older man, took Nancy aside into a separate room to question her. His intent was to determine if she was under duress of any kind to go through with this marriage. Impatient to make this official, I told Mrs. Cranmore that if he didn't bring her back out where I could see her and hear what was being said, I would _____ (expletive)! Mrs. Cranmore tried her best to calm down my 128 pounds of dynamite before I exploded. (Looking back, I realize that I really couldn't have made as big of an explosion as I gave myself credit for back then; I'm just saying.)

Finally, we completed the required process, and we were released. When we came out of the courthouse, I found I had a parking ticket under my windshield wiper! Just great! Finally, we made it through and left with our marriage license in hand, thanks to Mother Cranmore!

On June 14, 1963, Nancy and I were married, joined together in a ceremony at the same church that I grew up

17

in. Once called Bethel Temple, but by then, it was the Assembly of God (AOG) in Aubrey, Texas.

Reverend R. Y. Grimes[12] performed the ceremony, and our friend Pat Harmon played a song on the piano that was popular in the early 1960s, Floyd Cramer's now famous instrumental, "Last Date." We had our last date (as singles), but unlike the lyrics of the song, my dreams did come true, and our love affair would continue for the six decades of our lifetime of marriage.

Nancy had turned fourteen on March 18, and we got married on June 14, just six weeks after Carolyn and Kenneth were married. The other newlyweds were our Best Man and Matron of Honor.

We spent our first night together in a cheap motel in Lewisville, Texas. (Originally called Holford's Prairie, Lewisville dates back to the early 1840s.) That night, Nancy asked me what my intentions were for our life together. Although I was working as a carpenter at the time, I half-jokingly answered her, "Who knows? I might be a preacher someday." The Holy Spirit was still tugging at my heart and soul to preach the Gospel.

The next day, we drove down to Six Flags Over Texas and spent the day. Although it has become a now-famous theme park, at the time, all the rides were not yet up and running. What we did find, as we wandered around as newlyweds, was a set of fake wedding rings! We had married without rings, and there in the shop was a set of beautiful rings that looked like the real thing. I couldn't resist

Miss Cranmore, Gene P. King Exchange Vows

AUBREY (Special) — Miss Nancy Ruth Cranmor eand Gene Paul King were married June 14 at the Aubrey Assembly of God Church. After a brief wedding trip the couple will be at home in Aubrey.

Parents of the couple are Mr. and Mrs. E. F. Cranmore and Mr. and Mrs. W. I. King, all of Aubrey.

The Rev. R. L. Grimes officiated in the ceremony. Miss Pat Harmon presented traditional wedding selections at the organ.

The bride wore a lace over taffeta gown designed with a fitted bodice and a full, street-length skirt.

Mr. and Mrs. Kenneth Wilson, sister and brother - in - law of the bride, attended the couple

The bride attended Aubrey Hig

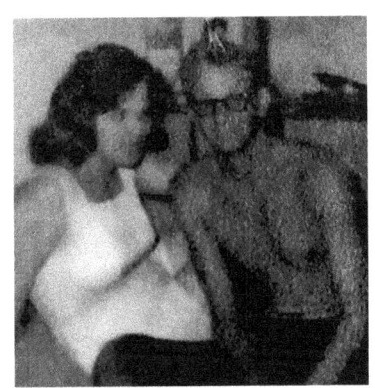

Miss Nancy Ruth Cranmore became the bride of Gene Paul King in an informal wedding at the Aubrey Assembly of God Church June 14 at 8 p.m. The Rev. R. Y. Grimes, pastor, officiated in the single ring ceremony. Miss Pat Harmon was organist and played the wedding march. The bride's costume was lace over taffeta designed with a fitted bodice draped collar, street length full skirt, paneled back.

Mrs. Kenneth Wilson was her sister's attendant and wore a blue taffeta dress. Kenneth Wilson, brother-in-law, was best man.

Parents of the couple are Mr. and Mrs. E. F. Cranmore and Mr. and Mrs. W. I. King of Aubrey. The bride attended Aubrey school and the bridegroom attended Pilot Point Gee High School and is employed by the L. Z. Harmon Construction Co. They are at home in Aubrey after a wedding trip to Dallas.

WEDDING RING SET PURCHASED
ON OUR HONEYMOON
AT SIX FLAGS OVER TEXAS

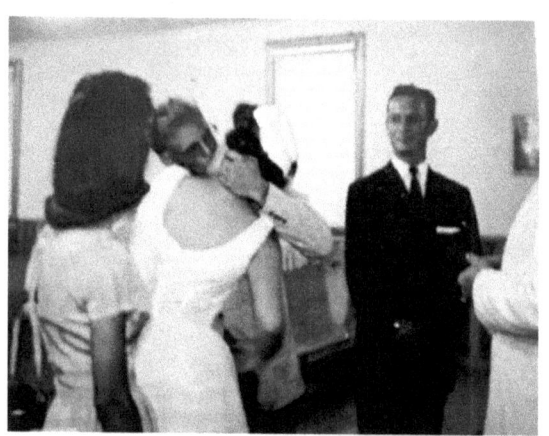

GENE AND NANCY KING - WEDDING KISS

getting them for my Nancy. I paid a whole sum of $5.00 for the set.

When we returned home from our short-lived honeymoon trip, she and I were at one of the local grocery stores in Aubrey when the owner's wife noticed Nancy's rings. She even called her husband up front to see the rings. She said, "No telling what those rings cost!" Neither of us had the heart to tell her what the rings really cost. My sweet Nancy wore them proudly—even though they did keep turning her finger green!

Newly Weds

Nancy and I started our life together on borrowed money and made payments of some kind for the rest of our married life. I realized from the very beginning that my woman was *top-shelf* (and that I was only *one* of the legs holding her shelf up). Nancy always put others before herself and never really realized her own true worth. But I knew, and so did The Almighty. Yes, I indeed married out of my league when I married Nancy Ruth Cranmore. Sweet Nancy was my counterbalance; she was extremely good at making me act (halfway) right most of the time. Some said I was henpecked and I just told them I loved the hen that was pecking. It could be that some of my jealousy through the years was an outward expression of my constant fear of losing her.

On top of working to support the family, our pastoral commitments required that I devote time to praying, studying the Word of God, preparing messages, visiting church members, praying for the sick, etc. We both did what was needed because nearly all the churches that she and I pastored were small and had very little financial support. I also must say that, man! It made me mad when we would attend rallies and fellowship meetings, and they referred to us as "part-time" pastors! We, indeed, were full-time pastors who also had to work a full-time outside job because of the limited resources at the churches we served!

My sweet Nancy took care of the home front, tending to whatever task was needed. God blessed Nancy and me with the most outstanding, beautiful, wonderful, and intelligent four children—plus ten grandchildren and ten (so far) great-grandchildren—in the whole wide world. I will have to give all the credit for raising our children to Nancy. For many years, I drove long distances to work an eight-hour workday plus an hour or so driving time each way, so I was often gone over ten to twelve hours a day. I must say, she did an amazing job, and I am so proud of all of our children!

As the years swiftly flew by and our children went their separate ways, Nancy still loved to cook, and she loved for the children and grandchildren to come on weekends for family meals together. She was so used to cooking for several people that when it narrowed down to just the two of us at home, she had to adjust the amount of food she needed to prepare. She always made buttermilk biscuits from scratch, and the first small batch she made for just the two of us didn't turn out so good, and, bless her heart, she cried. As much as I loved her buttermilk biscuits, I cried with her! But true to form, she could adapt, and as she narrowed it down, things began to look up at the Kings' table once again.

Our Golden Years

I've been talked about, criticized, looked down on, and God only knows what else, for what some people call "robbing the cradle" when I married Nancy Cranmore at the young age of fourteen. But let me tell you about my 14-year-old bride! She was very mature, not only in body but in mind as well. She cooked, sewed, and made dresses and shirts; she stitched and patched whatever needed to be fixed. She knew exactly where to place things, how to arrange our furniture, how to place lovely decorations, and hang pictures on our walls to make any house our home. She took care of me and my needs and raised our babies. She stayed hitched through both good and bad times. She and I entered our golden years together, celebrating sixty years of marriage. For those who would criticize, I would ask... *How did your marriage turn out, my friend?*

I must admit that from time to time, as God would move us from one place to another, there were times when Nancy would ask me, "Are you sure you've heard from God? Just how much have you prayed over this?" But most of the time, God would confirm the move within her heart, too. We lived in some places that were good to live in, and we lived in some places that were not so good to live in. Either way, Nancy made it a home for all of us. I remember that in one house that the church had provided for us, I had to cut wooden shims to level up the front of her china cabinet to keep the dishes from falling out! The floor was so uneven that walking across the floor was like riding the waves of the ocean.

In our latter years, Nancy loved to work on word puzzle books. She and I both loved to work on picture puzzles together. We would pick one out together at the store. When we started to work together putting the pieces together, I would pick out the border pieces. My sweet Nancy would usually have them put together by the time I'd finished finding them. She loved to be the one who could find the one piece that would be the hardest to find. I didn't mind her beating me, really, but what I didn't like was for her to keep rubbing it in! Of course, I'm just teasing. I would always fuss, but really, I loved to see the sparkle in her eyes when she beat me at anything we were doing.

I recall how Nancy was always afraid of heights. She rode in a small airplane once and began to get sick, so the pilot had to bring her down in a hurry. Because of that experience, she said, "Jesus said, 'Lo *(low)* I will be with you!'" I teasingly told her then that she and Jesus would have to work something out if she was going to be caught up in the rapture! She decided that she'd just stay on the ground until then because Jesus would take care of her whenever Gabriel blew the horn, and I should not worry about it! That was my sweet Nancy! I'm sure she's patiently waiting to rub it in on how she got to go to heaven before me.

Nancy was always the Queen of the King household. I may have been slow in learning some things about life. Still, I did realize that a happy wife makes a happy home— even if we never could agree on the thermostat setting in the house!

Chapter Two

The joining together of a poor, born-and-bred Texas boy and an equally poor, born-and-bred Oklahoma girl was a dream come true for me. With borrowed money in my pocket and the most beautiful and sweetest woman in the world standing beside me. I felt like I owned the whole wide world.

On our wedding day, Nancy had just turned fourteen, and I was just shy of twenty-one. I was nervous, and so was she because we both knew my older brothers and cousins were planning to really run us through the wringer as soon as our wedding ceremony was over. So, as soon as Nancy and I said our last vow and kissed. I grabbed her hand and pulled her so hard (to escape their planned shenanigans) that she literally came out of her shoes! There was a door opening into the older part of the church building, and we ran through it! We jumped into our car and drove away as Mr. & Mrs. Gene Paul King.

After our short honeymoon trip to Six Flags Over Texas, we came home to stay with my parents for a while. We had no furniture and no kitchenware, etc. We had nothing but our clothes and a heart full of love for each other; we were "living on love," as the old timers say!

The church I grew up in soon blessed us with a wedding shower, and my, oh my, some of the things the people gave us that night! Nancy had a little book, and she wrote down everyone's name and the gift they brought. We had several towels, several washcloths, dish towels, a bedspread, mixing bowls, two pillows; several blankets and sheets; a clothes basket, clothes pins, and a clothes pin bag; pots and potholders, a Corning Ware cooking set, a set of dishes, silverware, cake plate, set of glasses, a bathroom set, a pie plate, cookie jar, a flour sifter, and several gave us cash money. Man, alive! My Sweet Nancy had a sparkle in her eyes and was on cloud nine that night.

God blessed Nancy and me with our first child, Shannon Gene King, when Nancy was sixteen years old. Dr. McDonald delivered Shannon, and the doctor and hospital cost together was $250.00. My Sweet Nancy was a natural at being a good mother, and she still managed to keep our house clean and our meals on the table.

God blessed us with our second child, Anthony Paul King, when Nancy was eighteen years old. Dr. Gerald

Flanagan[13] delivered Anthony, and the doctor and hospital cost together was $275.00. (And I fussed over the $25.00 increase in the bill!) Both of our boys were born at the Denton Osteopathic Hospital on Highway 380 (old Highway 24) in Denton, Texas.

I saw from the very days of our marriage that Nancy was mature way beyond her age. She continued to show that maturity as, at just eighteen years old, she cared for our two small children while, at the same time, she did her best to keep everything running smoothly in our household.

So, we continued growing our family as God blessed us with our precious daughter, Regena Renee King, when Nancy was twenty years old. Dr. Lee delivered Renee at the old Flow Hospital in Denton. The hospital bill was $600.00, plus Dr. Lee's fee of $500.00.

Sweet Nancy, at just twenty years old, had a four-year-old, a two-year-old, and a newborn baby to care for, and still, she kept up with all the household chores. On top of caring for our children and doing household chores, Nancy would sometimes help her mother clean her house! Have I told you that she was sweet?

Nancy was thirty years old when God blessed us with our fourth child, Nathanael Paul King. Nathanael (Nathan) was also born at the old Flow Hospital (County Memorial) in Denton.[14] But this delivery wasn't as easy as the first three. They had to take the baby C-section before the full nine months was up. Dr. Rampolla delivered Nathan.

The hospital and doctor bill together were just a little over $4,000.00. My how things had increased from that first delivery!

Now, back to the births of our children. I don't know if you noticed the names of our children or not? Well, my name is **Gene Paul King**, and our firstborn son's name is Shannon **Gene** King.[15] Our second-born son's name is Anthony **Paul** King.[16] Our daughter's name is Re**gena** Renee King.[17] And our fourth child, our baby boy, is named Nathanael **Paul** King.[18] Yes, as you may have guessed already, I named them all while Nancy was still kind of out of it from giving birth. She would, from time to time, throw that up to me, especially since she really wanted to name our fourth child "Nathan Edward," after her dad, Edward Cranmore. What can I say? She was asleep when it was

30

time to name them. She loved me anyway because... **she was my sweet Nancy, Queen of all these Kings!**

Lighting Fires (of Several Kinds)

We soon moved from staying with my mom and dad to staying with Nancy's parents until we could rent a place of our own. After a few weeks we had saved enough money to rent a house on Lois Street (yes, it was named after my sister, Lois). As we were moving into our own home, I puffed up my manly chest in front of "my woman" and began to lay down the house rules. (*Wait for it...*)

Now, in my younger days, I usually wore Western-style shirts with the top two snaps undone. And I guess I had maybe three or four black hairs on my manly chest at that time. My sweet new bride smiled at me and my proclamation, then gently reached her hand inside my shirt, pulled my three or four black hairs out from beneath the shirt, and softly asked, "What was that you just said?" From that moment on, I knew I had my hands full with this lovely woman of mine.

Soon after we got our own house, a man and his wife parted ways, and that man offered to sell all their furniture to us for $250.00! It was a good deal for him (as he needed to sell it all) and a good deal for us. I had $50; I borrowed $100 from Nancy's dad. I borrowed another $100 from my brother-in-law, LZ Harmon.[19] Even though we were young, I did make sure the man wrote me a bill of sale as proof that I had bought all of their furniture and paid him in full that day. Man, was I glad I did that! Sure enough, within a month, the husband and wife had gotten back together and wanted all their furniture back. The man called and offered to give us our money back.

This man was a policeman, so he should have known that after he had given me a bill of sale for it all, by law, we didn't have to give anything back to them unless we wanted to do so. And we did not! After all, we had a house full of furniture for $250.00, and we intended to keep it. And we kept it with a clear conscience!

Now, my sweet Nancy—and she was sweet—set up and arranged the furniture just the way she wanted it, and she made our house into a home. I worked every day framing houses, and she worked every day keeping our house clean, our clothes clean and dry, and home-cooked meals on our table.

When we lived on Lois Street, we enjoyed watching the Oklahoma versus Texas football game on TV. Every time Oklahoma would make a touchdown, Nancy and her friend Sharon Baker (who lived three houses down and was also from Oklahoma) would get so fired up that they would run out in their front yards and cheer so loud that our neighbors would all look out to see what was going on!

In the meantime, Carl Baker (Sharon's husband) and I would stay inside with our heads bowed low and pouting. Both Nancy and Sharon were proud to be Okie's from Oklahoma!

Back when we all had a burn barrel in our backyards to burn our trash in, Nancy or Sharon (one or the other) would end up burning all the grass and weeds in the north end of town. The volunteer firefighters at our Fire Department got to know both women on a first-name basis! Each time a call came in, the firemen would bet on which one, Nancy or Sharon, had accidentally set the fire this time.

It was while we were living on Lois Street that God finally got my attention in a really big way. Neither Nancy nor I had been attending church, nor were we making any attempt to serve God. Even though we had some fun times, I was running from the call of God, and my life was mainly miserable. I sometimes would stay out late at night drinking with some of my friends downtown, leaving Nancy home to care for our babies all alone. I was very jealous of her and often stalked her like a hawk. Even though I could go out with friends whenever I wanted to, I didn't want her going anywhere by herself. I didn't want her to go shopping or anywhere without her mother or her sister or me going with her.

At this point in our lives only God knows why Nancy put up with and stayed with me. She had hinted a time or two that she was getting fed up with my drinking and staying out late, my jealous attitude, and the way I was treating her. But, foolishly, I continued. I went so far as to wipe my car tracks out of our driveway when I left the house so I could tell whether or not somebody had pulled into our driveway. It was sandy soil, and for that purpose alone, I wouldn't put gravel on our driveway. I smoked back then, and I'd check our ashtrays when I'd come home from work to see if any strange cigarette butts were in them. The bedspreads had better not be disturbed when I checked them.

I believe that satan knew God had great plans for Nancy and me further down life's highway, and he was trying his best to alter God's plan for our lives. At this time in my life, I was playing right into satan's hand. *I will tell you that only God and his mercy kept Nancy and me together during this time of our marriage!*

One day, my work got rained out on a job in Plano, Texas. So, I came home early. Although it was raining in Plano, it was dry and sunny in Aubrey. So, I sneaked up to our front door. It was open and our wood screen door was shut. I pulled on the screen door, and the screen door was latched. I looked inside and I saw baby Anthony sitting in his little walker and Shannon playing with a toy of some kind next to him.

About that time, I heard the back door open. I immediately ran and jumped over a four-foot chain link fence and had my fist doubled up, ready to hit whoever was coming out the back door. In my jealous mind I just knew that some man was in my house with my Nancy and was coming out of my back door.

True to form, it was sweet Nancy with a basket full of freshly washed clothes. She was headed for the clothesline to hang them out to dry. There were three steps she had to go down and she was on maybe the second step when she saw my fist headed toward her. Lucky for me, I stopped my swing before it struck her. She knew very well what I had been imagining in my mind. She dumped that basket of wet clothes on top of my head and began to cry.

"Gene Paul King, if you don't stop this, I'm taking my babies and leaving you for good. If I wanted to cheat and run around on you, you couldn't stop me. And, furthermore, you'd be the first one I'd tell if I was to cheat on you." She yelled at me, "I mean for you to stop it, you hear me? I mean, stop it! Stop making my life so miserable."

Saturday night, the 25th of November 1967, I had been downtown drinking with the boys and came home drunk. Shannon was about two and a half years old at the time, and Anthony was around six months old. Shannon was sick, coughing, and running a fever. Nancy had taken him during the day to see a doctor in Denton. The doctor had given him a shot of penicillin, not knowing that Shannon would be allergic to penicillin. Shannon had broken out in a rash and was still sick and crying. Nancy walked the floor holding Shannon and tending to baby Anthony, too, all day long and nearly all night *while I slept*.

I woke up Sunday morning with a hangover, but at least I got to sleep. I had planned to build a doghouse in our backyard, but Shannon was still sick and crying that morning, so Nancy brought him to me.

Just as I took him in my arms, **he stopped breathing.** And it seemed like almost immediately, his bowels released, his bladder emptied, and his body began to grow cold. I stood holding him in my arms, not really knowing what to do. Scared and trembling, I cried out for Nancy to come and help me. Seeing the child, she, too, looked stunned. In that terrifying moment, I knew one thing for sure... I had not been living for God, but we began to cry out to God anyway!

We had no telephone, but Nancy's sister had one, and she lived just four houses down from us. I held Shannon in my arms, and Nancy picked up baby Anthony. We began to run down the street as fast as we could. Once we arrived at her sister's house, Carolyn (who had just finished taking a course on CPR) began working with Shannon to get him to breathe. My brother-in-law Kenneth was immediately on the phone calling for an ambulance to come take us to a hospital in Denton. Finally, after about twelve minutes or so, Carolyn got Shannon to gasp for air, just a little bit every now and then.

Finally, fifteen minutes later, the ambulance arrived to take us to the hospital in Denton. The doctors at the Denton Osteopathic Hospital said they didn't know what to do, the baby was dying, and that we should get him to the Parkland Hospital in Dallas as quickly as we possibly could. We then had to call for another ambulance to come and take us to Parkland Hospital in Dallas. The Denton ambulance had us to the loading dock at Parkland Hospital in twenty-eight minutes. All the way from Denton to Dallas, Shannon would gasp for air every now and then.

Once we arrived, the doctors took him in immediately. They began to run tests and ask us all kinds of questions about medicines or home products he might have gotten into. Like the doctors in Denton, the Parkland doctors also admitted that they didn't really know what to do for him or what was wrong with him.

(Evidently, the allergic reaction to the penicillin caused his throat to swell, which prevented him from being able to breathe. Still, no one at that time seemed to know what the issue was or what to do about it.)

It was then I realized that man could only do so much. If God didn't perform a miracle or heal our baby, he'd die for sure. Parkland's emergency waiting room was packed. The whole place was crowded to capacity on that Sunday, November 26, 1967. I looked around, and I saw an ottoman (footstool). I didn't care who was watching me. I didn't care who was listening to me. I didn't care what anyone thought about me. I knew what I had to do. I knelt right there and used it as an altar.

First off, I began to repent for my sins. Then I said,

> "Dear God, if this is what it takes to get me to do what you've called me to do, Lord, I am willing and ready to do it. But Almighty God, if you could see fit to give us our baby back, please do so. But if you choose to take him home with you, dear Lord, you'll have to give Nancy and me

grace enough and strength enough to carry
on with our lives."

The doctors admitted Shannon to the hospital that
Sunday night. They moved him from the emergency room
to the eighth floor. We were so close to Dallas' Love Field
(an airport) that we could see the airplanes taking off and
landing from the window next to Shannon's bed. The doctor had Shannon placed under a vaporized oxygen tent for
the night and told us that he didn't know anything else to
do for Shannon. He also told us that if Shannon were to
make it through the night, he would ask a team of doctors
to come in and examine him thoroughly and do their best
to find out what was going on with his tiny body.

Meanwhile, both Nancy and I had been praying. We
both dedicated our lives to God and vowed to do whatever
He asked us to do. Reaching out for support, Nancy called
my parents, who had gone to Louisiana to visit Dad's sister. My parents said they would leave immediately and be
at Parkland Hospital by nine o'clock that night.

When my parents arrived, the very first thing that my
mother asked me was, "Son, have you made things right
with God?" I assured her that I had. Then she said to me
what I have never forgotten, "Your baby is going to be
alright."

This is the woman who raised me. I knew from experience that my mom had her "royal telephone" connected
to God's main line! Growing up, I saw and heard her pray

over dogs, chickens, cats, cows, horses, and pigs, and, for sure, she prayed for all of us kids! I witnessed prayer after prayer answered when my mother prayed. I remember the time that some of our chickens stopped laying eggs. My mother took the bottle of olive oil and walked around the chicken house. She sloshed olive oil on the old boards of the chicken house while she prayed, telling God that some of the hens were not doing their part and that our family needed more eggs. The next day, there were twice the number of eggs!

This is the woman who raised me and who came to tell us, "Your baby is going to be alright." The following day, the doctors came in looking for the King's baby. We pointed to Shannon and said, "Here he is." They replied, "Oh, no [as in, it can't be him]. The King's baby is very ill." But there was Shannon, standing up, holding his bed rail, watching the planes come and go at Love Field. *God had performed a miracle on him overnight!*

They finally realized that he, indeed, was the King's baby. They checked him over from head to toe. They said we didn't know what was wrong with him when you brought him in, and we don't see anything wrong with him now. Then they began to warn us that when oxygen has been cut off from the brain for several minutes, like in Shannon's case, he might still suffer some brain damage. I replied, "God didn't roll back the waters of the Red Sea to take the children of Israel halfway across and then drown them. No, He saw them safely to the other side."

The doctors then told us that the One who made our baby well could take care of him at our house, too. The hospital dismissed Shannon on Monday afternoon and wrote on the top of the chart, "Miracle, act of God."

And Parkland Hospital never sent us a bill. That has to be another "miracle, act of God."

As for residual brain damage? God did not stop short of complete healing. After Shannon started school, he earned A's (well, until he discovered girls and then his grades dropped somewhat for a while). At the time of the writing of this book, Shannon Gene King is fifty-nine years old, lives in Texas, and has worked long-term in the construction and drywall industry; he has worked for the same company for more than twenty-five years and is a Field Superintendent over all construction. **Miracle, act of God.**

Chapter Three

Soon after, we were home from the hospital with Shannon, Nancy, and I let Jesus know He was welcome not only in our hearts but that He was welcome in our home, too. Prayer and scripture reading all at once became part of our everyday lives. A sudden hunger to be in church and fellowship with God's people reigned within our hearts. Indeed it was Jesus who saved us and our marriage, too.

As mentioned previously, I was raised in a Pentecostal church (by denomination) and saved as a small lad. I felt the call of God on my life at the early age of eight, but I drifted away from God as I grew into my teen years. However, being raised in a Pentecostal church does not automatically mean you're Pentecostal. You are not Pentecostal until you have experienced the power of Pentecost in your own life. So, I determined within my heart that I must earnestly seek to be baptized and filled with the Baptism of the Holy Ghost. I believed that this was the answer to overcome the temptations and roadblocks satan had been and would be placed in front of me.

As I began to seek to be filled with the Holy Ghost, I started going up to the church every night to pray after I came home from work. Our pastor, Brother Grimes, Brother Otto Wilson[20], and Elder Pat Burchett[21] would come to the church and pray with me. Elder Burchett was 86 at the time, but these men would still come almost every night to pray with me.

It was one of those nights while I was praying and seeking God at the altar that two men's faces came before me. They were a same-sex couple with whom I had previously had a run-in on a remodeling job.

Seeing their faces before me in prayer, I remembered the couple and the incident right away. I was helping to remodel their house, and the more effeminate male told me to relocate a window. While I was in the process of moving the window, the more masculine partner saw what I was doing and asked why I was doing it. I explained that his partner had requested that I move it. When the effeminate partner saw that his partner didn't seem to want the window moved, suddenly, he said he did not tell me to do it! The masculine of the two men began to curse at me and ordered me off their property. As I was gathering up my tools, I assured them that the first time I caught either of them or both together off their property, I would give both a good whipping. I had ill feelings within my heart for some time against those two men.

When their faces appeared before me as I prayed, the Holy Spirit, speaking to my inner ear, said I needed to ask them to forgive me for the hate I had carried in my heart against them. I said, "Lord, they wronged me; I didn't wrong them." And the Spirit speaking to my inner ear (God's unmistakable voice that one hears inside, instead of an external audible voice that others could hear also) said, "They're not trying to get closer to me, but you are!" I understood then that this hatred in my heart was preventing that.

I told those who were praying with me that night that I'd be back in a little while and that I had to go and do something that God wanted me to do. As I was driving out to the two men's house, the old devil kept telling me that as soon as they would see who I was, one of them would smart off, and I'd hit him. Then what would I do? But I was determined to do as the Holy Spirit directed me and ask them to forgive me.

I knocked on their door, and the effeminate partner answered the door. He had earrings on his ears, lipstick on his lips, and was dressed in a bathrobe. He asked me what I was doing, why I was there, and what I wanted. I answered that I needed to talk to him and his partner. He left and returned to the door with his partner. I said to them both, "Fellows, I've just recently gotten saved, and I've been seeking for the Baptism of the Holy Ghost. Tonight, while I was praying, your faces came before me. And I've come to ask you both to forgive me for all the ill feelings and hatred I've had in my heart against you."

Tears began to roll down both of their cheeks. They both stepped outside and gave me a big hug. I hurriedly drove back to the church and I just knew that God would baptize and fill me with the Holy Ghost that night. But, no, it didn't happen that night. But I did feel a sweeter spirit within my heart and soul anyway.

Our church began a revival on January 21, 1968, with Evangelist Travis Bates and his wife. Brother Travis was the nephew of Brother A. C. Bates. I just knew I'd be filled with the Holy Ghost in the Sunday morning service. No, it didn't happen then, either. Neither did it happen that Sunday night. Monday night, I prayed at the altar for over an hour, and I said everything some of the ones praying with me told me to say.

One lady said she was saying Hallelujah over and over when she got filled with the Holy Ghost. So off I went, saying "Hallelujah" over and over. Then another one praying with me said they were saying "Glory, glory" over and over when they received. So I changed to saying, "Glory, glory" over and over. Tuesday night brought the same thing, over and over. Wednesday night, here we went again with the same thing. Meanwhile, a lady who had just married and moved to Aubrey from West Texas was attending the revival. This lady had no trouble receiving the baptism of the Holy Ghost. Early in the week, she was filled and baptized with the Holy Ghost, with the evidence of speaking in tongues. There I was, still seeking. So, I got a little mad about that. I said, "God, I was raised in this church, and I feel that I should have been filled and baptized with the Holy Ghost first. But, instead, you've filled and baptized her with the Holy Ghost first!" The Holy Spirit gave me a pretty good whipping (attitude correction) that night and showed me that I was still a work in progress!

On that Thursday night, January 25, 1968, when the Evangelist called for those seeking to be filled and baptized with the Holy Ghost to come to the altar, I reached and took the baby (Anthony) out of Nancy's arms and told her to go on to the altar if she wanted to go. I didn't really want to go to the altar that night, so I used holding the baby as my excuse for not going to the altar. Sister Wilma Wilson[22] (my Sunday School teacher when I was a child) came to me and said, "Give me the baby and get yourself to that altar." Stalling, I looked her in the eye and said, "The baby wants me to hold him tonight." Not to be dissuaded, she looked me back in the eye, smiled, and said, "That baby can't even talk!" With that, she quickly pulled him from my arms and pointed me toward the altar.

I slowly started walking toward the altar. That night, I had on an old pair of Tony Llama cowboy boots that had gaping holes in the soles of both boots. It was impossible to kneel and keep the bottom of both feet flat on the floor (so that the holes didn't show), so I just stood straight up. I had so many thoughts running through my mind at that time. Finally, I began to pray, "Thank you, Jesus, for all that you have already done for me and my family. Thank you, Jesus, thank you, Jesus!" About that time my tongue felt as big as a fist. I felt the power of the Holy Spirit hit me from the top of the head all the way down to the holes in the bottom of my boots!

I began to speak in an unknown language, and as I began to look around, I saw Uncle LH Kruger[23] standing right in front of me, grinning like an opossum eating ripe persimmons. I shouted and kicked up my heels, not letting the holes in my boots bother me anymore! My life changed forever that night. Nancy was also filled with the Holy Ghost in that same revival.

I spoke in tongues the rest of that night and nearly all the following day without stopping. I began to get a little worried when I woke up the following day still speaking in tongues, so I drove up to Brother Grimes' house and knocked on the door. Sister Charlotte Grimes[24] answered the door and just stood there for a moment, then smiled at me and invited me in. She had me sit on their couch. I sat there just chattering away. Soon, Brother Grimes looked around the doorway with shaving cream all over his face, smiled, and said he would be right with me. I thought it was strange that neither he nor Sister Grimes seemed to be upset or bothered about my jabbering away in tongues. I just sat there on the pastor's couch, jabbering away. Eventually, after Brother Grimes had finished shaving, he came in and assured me that everything was alright. He told me that the Holy Spirit was speaking through me, and things would soon return to being normal once again.

Evangelist Travis Bates and his wife were staying at the Grimes' house. It wasn't long before Brother and Sister Bates also looked around the corner and smiled really big. Brother Bates hollered out, "Praise God!"

After I finally surrendered to the call of God to preach His Word, I received my Exhorter Permit with the Assemblies of God that same year. Many of my friends began to tell me that I had to go to Bible College if I was going to be a preacher. I told them that I didn't see how when I already had two children and had to work every day to provide for my family. I prayed earnestly and sincerely over this matter. One evening, while I was praying in our bedroom, the Lord spoke to me again through my inner ear that He would educate me, and from that day forward, God placed people in my life who would ask me questions that kept me studying the Word to find the answers. People that I crossed paths with would teach me things that I needed to know as a preacher.

God began to do a work in Nancy's life, too. Her relationship with Sister Grimes helped prepare and equip her to be a preacher's wife. She grew in knowledge and wisdom. She learned to discern when she was needed and how to help at the right place and at the right time. Sister Grimes was an excellent example for Nancy to learn from and set the bar high for a pastor's wife. Brother Grimes taught me many things as well. I will always be thankful that I was brought up under his ministry.

Nancy and I were just getting over our experience with Shannon's hospital ordeal when Anthony came down with a nasty ear infection. My sister Lois' first baby had died from an ear infection that had drained inward to its brain, so fear of that possibility gripped both Nancy and me. We took turns holding Anthony in our arms, walking the floor, and praying for God to heal our baby. After many hours, both of us were tired, sleepy, and worn out. We decided to go out to my mother's house so she could help with the baby and also help us pray!

My mother took Anthony in her arms and began to walk the floor and pray. In the meantime, Nancy, who was utterly worn out, soon fell asleep. I went into the kitchen and poured a cup of coffee. As I began to drink my coffee, for no particular reason at all, I said, "God, if you heal our baby, I will never drink another cup of coffee as long as I live." I saw that Mother had a promise box sitting on her table. I reached over and pulled out a Scripture promise, and this is what it said:

> I have heard thy prayer. I have seen thy tears.
> Behold, I will heal thee. (2 **Kings** 20:5)

At that moment, baby Anthony stopped crying, and his little ear began to drain outward. From that night on, I've never had another cup or drop of coffee. The Bible teaches us that it's better to not even make a vow than it is to make a vow and not keep it!

> *When you make a vow to the Lord your God, you shall not delay to pay it*, for the Lord your God will surely require it of you, and it would be sin to you. But if you abstain from vowing, it shall not be sin to you. *That which has gone from your lips you shall keep and perform*, for you voluntarily vowed to the Lord your God what you have promised with your mouth. (Deuteronomy 23: 21–23 NKJV; emphasis added)

It wasn't long until Nancy and I were voted in to be our church's Christ's Ambassador leaders. We were blessed with several couples and several singles in our Christ's Ambassadors services from time to time. We would have our youth service at 6:00 p.m. every Sunday, and the primary church service would start an hour later. On many Sundays, God would move in our youth services and spill over into the primary services, with God continuing to move in a mighty way.

Any time we heard of a revival within driving distance, Nancy would have supper on the table and the kids ready so that as soon as I'd come home from work and get cleaned up, we could eat dinner. Then, we would load up the kids, and away we'd go! Most of the time, Nancy and the kids would sleep while I drove back home. I was young and strong in my body, so I could still function with very little sleep back then.

Once a month, the Section would have a Christ's Ambassadors rally, and our group would almost always attend and be blessed. Also, once a month, there would be a Sectional Fellowship meeting for all the churches, and we would go to those as well. It seemed like Nancy and I couldn't stay away from God's house in those early years of our walk with Christ.

We realized that "faith comes by hearing, and hearing by the word of God" (Romans 10:17). Each church service increased our faith and trust in God. As I look back at our beginning, I can now see how God was educating me precisely as He said He would. In every church service we attended, I gained new knowledge and understanding of His Word.

When asked what Bible College I graduated from, I'd tell them, "I attended the college of a worn-out church pew, got a degree in *KNEEology* at an old-fashioned altar, and studied tirelessly in the pages of my well-worn Bible." I'm not putting down anyone who does have the time and finances to go to Bible College—by no means! It's just that in my own situation, family-wise, I didn't have enough money or enough time! But God has carried me through every roadblock that satan placed in front of me.

I remember well the first sermon I preached way back in 1968. It was at our home church in Aubrey, Texas. I preached from the book of John, chapter 15. My text was entitled "Jesus, the True Vine." It lasted at least ten minutes before I ran out of anything to say. The first time I was invited to preach outside my home church was at the First Assembly of God (now named Crossroads Church) in Whitesboro, Texas, with Pastor Ernest Smith. He was the first pastor to ask me to preach outside of my home church. This time, I preached for at least fifteen minutes before I ran out of anything to say!

I stood beside Pastor Smith at the end of the service, shaking hands with people as they were leaving the church. This one elderly lady shook my hand and said, "Enjoyed your little talk, sonny boy." Brother Smith got a big laugh out of it, and I've never forgotten what she said, either.

In 1969, Nancy and I tried out for the pastorate at the First Assembly of God in Whitewright, Texas. The church at that time had nine voting members, and most of those nine were on limited-income social security. We preached the Sunday morning service and the Sunday night service. After the Sunday night service, they asked our family to stand outside on the front walk of the church while they voted on us! This really tall man with a deep voice came out on the sidewalk with us and just stood there for a while. Then, he said, "I'm sorry." (Right then, a huge lump came up in my throat.) Breaking into a smile, he then said, "You got all nine votes!"

When we moved to Whitewright, Texas, I was 28 years old, Nancy was 21, Shannon was 5, Anthony was 3 years old, and Renee was just 1 year old. The church did have an old house next to the church for us to live in, but most of the plumbing had to be reworked before the washing machine could be used. The church's tithes on the first of the month were always about $60.00. The rest of the month, Sunday offerings added up to maybe $10.00 or $20.00. Needless to say, I had to hold an outside job to provide for our family. I drove 136 miles round-trip every weekday to my job in Mesquite, Texas.

I was helping Nancy clean the church one Saturday, and I happened to find the ballots where they had voted for us. One ballot was marked in red ink, and I guess that person had a hard time making up his or her mind because it had yes, no, yes, no, and yes written on it. We must have been lucky that day because the last space to write in had a yes in it!

We hadn't been there very long when one Saturday, I got a call from one of the businessmen downtown who asked me if I was the pastor of First Assembly. I assured him I was, and then he said, "You'd better come down here!" I asked him what for, and he replied that one of my church members had a claw hammer and was chasing one of her boys down the sidewalk, yelling, "I'm going to kill him!"

As quickly as I could, I drove to the downtown area, and sure enough, the battle was on. I confronted the mother first about the uproar. She started telling me all the things that her son had done. When I finally got her to stop and listen, I said to her, "In the middle of downtown with all the townspeople watching is not the proper place to carry on like this, now is it? It's not the Christian thing to do. All the townspeople will judge our whole congregation by what is going on here with you and your son." With that commotion as one of my first introductions to the townspeople, we were off to an eventful start pastoring in our new hometown.

Our home church pastor, Brother Grimes, came to preach a revival at the First Assembly of God in Whitewright. On the first night of the revival, I introduced him as the man responsible for every argument that Nancy and I ever had because he was the one who married us! Brother Grimes calmly walked to the pulpit, and before he began to preach, he said, "I never married either one of them. I only performed the wedding ceremony!" That loosened everyone up, and we had an excellent revival with Brother Grimes.

One Sunday morning, just as I was starting to preach, a young lady came down front and asked me to pray for her because she had a bad migraine headache. I got the olive oil, anointed her forehead, and put the lid back on the bottle. I turned around and closed my eyes to pray. As I barely touched her forehead, she fell over backward! Being so young in the Lord, I never had such a thing happen to me.

There is an old country song, "The Gambler," sung most famously by American country singer Kenny Rogers, with lyrics that said, "You've got to know when to hold 'em, know when to fold 'em, know when to walk away, know when to run!" Well, at that moment, I didn't quite know what I should do!

I just kept praying and encouraged the people to keep praying and praising the Lord! In a few minutes, the young lady stood up and began to testify that her headache was gone! Thank you, Lord, for the learning experiences that You've given this little ole' preacher from Aubrey, Texas.

Another time, there was a lady who moved to White-wright and then started calling different people from the church asking questions about me and my family. We had a phone, but she never would call us! After a week or two, I began to wonder what was going on with all the calling of the different ones of the church but never calling us. One day, we got rained out from work, and I got home early. So, I told Nancy I was going to find this woman and see just what her problem was.

I got her phone number from one of our church members and called to see if she and her husband were home. (I always found this out before visiting, and if the husband was not at home, I would take Nancy or someone else with me. I made it my practice to never visit females without Nancy or others present.) She told me that her husband was indeed at home, so I drove over to their residence.

When I arrived at the residence, I knocked on the door, introduced myself, and was invited inside. The woman began to tell me that she was a prophet and that God sent her to Whitewright like he sent Jonah to Nineveh. I listened as she continued on to say that God had sent her to Whitewright to warn the people that he was going to destroy one side of the town. I stood listening to her professing to be sent by the Spirit of God and claiming to be a prophet. Yet, the woman in front of me was wearing her blouse unbuttoned halfway down the front! My spirit was by no means bearing witness with her spirit that she was a prophet sent from God.

As she was speaking, her husband came into the room, rolling himself into the room in his wheelchair. He let me know right up front that he was not a Christian. Oddly enough, in the middle of this crazy story, the husband said that he would like for me to pray with him before I left that he would be saved! I was certainly willing to pray with the man. Still, his wife butted in to inform me that her husband could not be saved until he confessed everything that he and another woman had done. Evidently, he had left this wife for a time to live with another woman, and the wife wanted to know everything, all the details. She again informed me that God could not and would not save him unless he confessed everything to her.

Ignoring her objections, I knelt on my knees in front of her husband's wheelchair. I looked him straight in the eyes, and I said, "Sir, you only need to confess your sins to the One who can forgive you and cleanse you of your sins. And his name is Jesus."

Then I asked him if he was ready to pray, and he said he was. As he and I started to pray, she interrupted us. After several attempts and interruptions, her husband finally prayed through to being born again.

By this time, I had been gone so long that Nancy had got worried and came to check on me. She drove over to see if I was alright, but before Nancy could get out of the car, the lady ran out and began to tell her that I had confessed to her a lot of bad things that I had done! Her husband told Nancy not to believe anything that his wife might have told her because he thought she may be demon-possessed! It was quite an exciting day for us! Again, I had to say, "Thank you, Lord, for another learning experience."

Although the Whitewright church had only those nine voting members when we became pastors, with the Lord's hand on us in the work, the church began to grow. We started to attract more and more visitors who were moving in from out of town. (Thankfully, they were not all like the lady who thought she was a deliverance prophet.)

One of the more humorous tales from our time pastoring in Whitewright was when a visiting couple noticed that I had a front tooth missing. However, not only did I have a front tooth missing, but so did three other men in the church at that time! After Sunday morning service, the couple came over to shake my hand and said how much they enjoyed the service. The man asked (only half-jokingly) if having a front tooth pulled was a ritual of some sort in order to be a member of the church! We all laughed and assured him that all of us having our front teeth missing at the same time was purely a coincidence and they would certainly be welcome with all their teeth intact.

In addition to the humorous, our church also experienced the miraculous. Once, a family of five moved into the area whose father was an airplane pilot for Braniff Airlines. His wife was a Holy Ghost woman of great faith. The couple had three young daughters whose first names all started with the letter "H." The father was making good money at the airlines at that time, so they borrowed the money to purchase an old farm with a two-story farmhouse.

The drawback on the farm was that the mortgage on the farm required them to make huge monthly payments. And, soon after purchasing it, Braniff suddenly laid off over four hundred pilots! This father was one of those who was suddenly without a job. The family was in danger of losing the farm and everything they owned. Finally, after three or so months of being out of work, he got a job, but it required that he stay out of town all week long. He was only able to come home to his family on the weekends.

One week, while he was away at work, in the middle of winter, the heating unit in the farmhouse broke. The wife called the repair man to see if it could be fixed. They were already strapped for money because of the layoff, and the report on the heater was not good. The heating unit in the old farmhouse was ancient, and a particular part had gone out on the lower part of the unit. The repairman didn't know of any place that would stock the part or if the type and size of bearing that was needed was even still manufactured.

That Holy Ghost-filled woman with great faith prayed over their non-working heating unit. Then, she turned it on again. It began to run smoothly as silk with no problem at all! She called us and asked us to come and see what God had done! Thank you, Jesus, for another learning experience!

Another family that attended the Whitewright church had two young boys. The boys still lived at home and came to church almost every service. This same family also had two married daughters. One of the boys told me on Sunday morning that their brother-in-law was coming to church that night to give me a good thrashing (for some unknown reason). Well, now, guess what? That Sunday evening, just as I opened up my Bible to read the Scripture, that big brother-in-law of theirs walked into church.

I looked back his way, and there he sat with both thumbs stuck in his ears, waving his hands up and down, sticking out his tongue like a small kid. Then he held up a finger... to let me know he was number one, I guess (grin).

I closed my eyes and began to silently pray, "Jesus, you called me to preach the Word, and Jesus, that is exactly what I'm going to do. Jesus, you take care of that idiot back there making gestures in front of all the people here in Your house." I opened my eyes, and guess what? He was gone. I never knew what his problem was.

That same man (the crazy brother-in-law) one day told his father-in-law that he was going to kill his wife (the daughter). Then he said that he was going to come over to the father-in-law's house, come in, sit down, and start watching television in their living room. He mocked him, saying that no one would even suspect anything was wrong.

The day came when the crazy brother-in-law did exactly what he said he was going to do. He beat his wife to death in front of their small children and then carried her body out to an old abandoned well in the middle of a field. The law officers like to have never found her body. The funeral home had her body frozen in a zipped-up bag. They encouraged everyone that the graveside service could not last very long or we would all regret it because the smell would come out from the zipped-up bag.

She was buried next to her sister, who had died from a train accident some time ago. After the graveside service was over, the father pointed to the two graves of his daughters and asked me to explain the verse, "And we know that all things work together for good to them that love God..." (Romans 8:28). He wondered what good he was supposed to get from that as he pointed to the two graves again.

Up until that time, I was confident that I could answer just about any question about the Bible that could be asked. This was different. After giving it some thought, I said, "I can't explain it. But I can point you to the one who can, and His name is Jesus." Silently, I said between myself and the Lord, "Thank you, Jesus, for yet another educational experience."

We had a mother and daughter who started attending church, but the husband never came to church with them. I learned that he was a professional gambler who gambled in places like Florida, Las Vegas, New Orleans, etc. Whenever I knew this man was in town, I tried to visit him and witness to him. Often, he would say, "Some day, preacher! Someday, I'll surprise you and come to church and give my heart and life to God."

Even though he wouldn't attend service, there were many times when he was a big winner that he would send a lot of money with his wife to be given as tithes to the church. One month, when the church was running low on finances, my sweet Nancy asked if it would be wrong for her to pray that the gambling man would have some big wins.

Nancy and I (being young in the Lord and pastoring our first church) received a lot of super holy advice from a lot of "super holy" people. Some of these would say, "Our church shouldn't receive the gambling money if we know it is gambling money!" Well, after much thought and prayer, I read through the Scriptures where God had instructed Moses to tell the children of Israel to borrow all the gold and silver from the Egyptians to take with them on their journey to the Promised Land. I finally concluded that there would be nothing wrong with accepting money regardless of where it came from as long as we used it for

His glory and for His kingdom! (I noticed that those same "super holy" ones never seemed concerned about giving nor about us when the church was only giving us as a family just $10.00 to $20.00 a week to live on! So, I am just saying.)

Carl's Sausage Company was in the city of Whitewright. On a specific day of the week, they would slaughter the pigs. You could hear them squealing all over town and the countryside. Their slogan was, *"We are a whole-hog business! We put everything in the sausage but the squeal."* It took us a good while to get used to those loud squeals. But they did have internationally award-winning sausage![25]

The largest grocery store in Whitewright was owned and operated by a man from my hometown. Every time Nancy went to the grocery store, the owner would tell her to tell me to be sure and visit the hardware store downtown. He kept insisting that I should visit, so one stormy, rainy day, I decided to visit the hardware store and see why my hometown friend was so eager for me to do so.

As I walked up to the open doorway to the hardware store, I could see several men inside, some playing dominoes, some playing cards, and others playing checkers. Just as I stepped inside the door opening, I heard a voice say, "What are you looking for, you four-eyed (expletive)!" Man, oh, man! My blood began to boil. I looked around to see which one of the older men was doing the talking, but all of them had their heads bowed and were trying not to laugh out loud. Just then, the same voice began to curse at me again. I looked behind me to find that the owner of the store had a big old parrot perched on a pedestal. It was the parrot that was doing all the trash-talking! I then understood why my friend who owned the grocery store wanted me to visit the hardware store downtown! What a sense of humor he had.

After Nancy and I left the First Assembly of God in Whitewright, I received word that they had elected a new pastor. I drove over one day so that I could carry him over to meet the gambling man. I encouraged the new pastor to continue to visit and pray for the gambling man because I believed that God would someday save him.

It was about six months later that the gambling man's wife called and said, "Brother King, you'll not believe

FIRST ASSEMBLY OF GOD, WHITEWRIGHT TX
(PHOTO FROM 2024)

what happened this morning at church!" Of course, I quickly replied, "Your husband got saved?" She said, "No, but please hear me out." She told me that her husband had, indeed, finally come to church. As he was coming in the front door of the church, the new pastor greeted him and noticed that the husband had a package of cigarettes in his front shirt pocket. The pastor stopped him right there and told him not to come inside and defile God's house with his cigarettes in his shirt pocket! She said that her husband looked at the pastor, shook his head, grinned, turned around, and walked right out. He went back to his pickup truck and drove back home. She said, "He'll never ever come back to that church again."

The Bible says, "Open rebuke is better than secret love" (Proverbs 27:5). After I prayed, I called the pastor. With a heart of love and compassion, I asked him why he did what he did and what he had said when the gambling man finally came to church. Instead of replying, the pastor hung up the phone! Then he called the Sectional Presbyter. The Presbyter called me and informed me that I no longer pastored the First Assembly of God in Whitewright and that I was not to interfere with anything pertaining to any of the church's people ever again.

Well, so much for trying to help! I still feel that there were more ways than one to look at that situation, and I know there were definitely better ways to welcome the gambling man who had finally made the decision to come to church!

Chapter Four

In 1971, Nancy and I rented a house back in Aubrey, Texas. That same year, Dad and Mom bought us a one-acre lot in Country Estates (which is now Krugerville). Nancy and I took out a loan from Pilot Point National Bank and built a four-bedroom brick home on the one-acre lot. We lived there and attended the Tioga Community Church (an AOG church) for about two years until we felt led by God to reopen the First Assembly of God in Howe, Texas.

In June of 1969, the First Assembly of God in Howe, Texas, was founded by Rev. Jim Uselton. The original church was started in an old Presbyterian church, which was over one hundred years old at that time. It was on the corner of Denny and Haning, where the Independent Bank now stands. They bought the church for $5,500 and made payments of $55 per month. Rev. Uselton was self-employed in the construction business while pastoring the church until June 1971. Rev. Virgil Miller and Rev. Joseph Wilson pastored the church during the early 1970s until the church closed for some time.[26]

Early in the year 1973, Nancy and I, with all our children, moved to Howe to reopen that church and the old building. (I will get more into on the old building in a moment.) Nancy and I were the fourth pastors to attempt to make a go of it with the church in Howe. I was 31, Nancy was 24, Shannon was 8, Anthony was 6, and Renee was 4 years old. There was no parsonage, so we rented a house just as you go into Howe on Highway 5, on the right-hand side of the road. We were in that house for about a year and a half.

During this early time pastoring in Howe, groceries were "slim pickens" (very limited) in the Kings' household. The lady who was the Section Leader for the WMC (Women's Missionary Council) called and asked me if I would come and preach at next month's sectional rally. I told her to let me pray about it, and I'd get back with her to let her know. I wanted to preach at a Sectional Fellowship meeting, but I did not really want to preach to a bunch of old ladies! Nancy came in and asked what the call was all about. When I told her, she looked at me and said, "You need to pray, alright! Pray through and call her back! Let her know you'll be more than glad to preach to a bunch of old ladies."

Little did I know that God had laid it on the Section Leader's heart to send cards out to all the other churches and ask them to bring a grocery pounding for our family! If you don't know what that is, that's when every person brings a pound of something—some form of staple, groceries, or supplies—to bless the family. Nancy always tried to steer me right. When God gave me Nancy, sweet and fancy, He gave me the best of the best!

Now, my friends, I don't want to leave the impression that my sweet Nancy was perfect and always right all the time. For instance, I remember one specific Communion Sunday in our history of pastoring. When the people partook of the communion cup, everyone all over the church began to frown. Then I swallowed mine, and I knew why. Nancy had used cranberry juice instead of grape juice! She was the one who bought it and poured it. She still said it was my fault. Imagine that!

Sometime in 1975, we moved just a few miles away to a rented one-story home in the nearby small town of Dorchester. While living in Dorchester, we had a nasty winter, and I was unable to work at my construction jobs. Without work and a steady paycheck, our electricity was eventually disconnected for non-payment. Since the house was all electric, we had no lights, no refrigerator, and no working stove to cook meals on. It was a tough time for our family.

I knew, somehow, we had to make provisions to at least enable Nancy to cook for the family. So, I went to a man in the area who was quite wealthy to ask for a loan to get our electricity back on. The man refused to help. He told me that if I was in the will of God, the Lord would never have allowed our electricity to be turned off!

Thankfully, Nancy's Dad brought us two big old Caterpillar batteries and a couple of DC light bulbs so that we could have lights. A friend brought us a Coleman camp stove for Nancy to cook on, along with several extra fuel containers for the camp stove. The house had an old fireplace, so the kids and I gathered up tree limbs, old pieces of wood, and anything else that would burn so that we could at least keep one room of the house warm. We used an ice chest to keep our perishable food items cold. Through it all, only a few close friends (and God) knew about our situation that winter. There was no point in concerning others, as most of our close friends were as poor as we were and in no position to help. We later moved to a house on Duke Street in Howe and remained there until we left the First Assembly of God in Howe.

Now, back to the church building. When we arrived, the Denton Section of the Assemblies of God allowed us to reopen in the old church building located next to the (then) Howe State Bank. The structure was built in the late 1800s and was not at all plumbed or square—in fact, it leaned about five inches to the north! As I said, it was originally a Presbyterian church, and it still had the old pews in the sanctuary. Over time, random passers-by had come in from the street to use the restrooms, filling the toilets to the brim with no water in them to flush the waste. It was a terrible sight, and the smell was even worse! Nancy and I had to wear masks and rubber gloves to clean the toilets. Even after a good cleaning, the restrooms were quite smelly for some time. Welcome to the glamorous life of pastoring! Thank you, Lord, for yet another educational experience.

As soon as the inside was usable, we made contact with a young couple and their two small children who had previously attended the church before its closing. They started back, and the lady volunteered to play the piano as we sang a few hymns for our first service. Then, I sat on the old wooden altar rail, and we had Bible study. The four people in that family and the five in ours made up the nine in attendance for our first church service and the re-opening of the First Assembly of God in Howe.

Even though we were still growing, we wanted to have an AOG Christ's Ambassadors rally in Howe. Since our little church building was not big enough to hold the rally, we got permission from the Howe School System to use the High School football stadium for the rally. The night of the Christ's Ambassadors rally, we had the pulpit set out on the football field.

The AOG Section Leader for all the region's Christ's Ambassadors groups was in charge of the music, so he had selected someone to sing before the ministry speaker came forward. I will tell you what! That man could not carry a tune in a bucket! Yet, there he was, in the stadium, trying to lead the singing that night! We were *not* off to a great start.

As I walked around, I saw that several of the Howe High School students had come, but they were sitting in cars, listening and laughing. My heart was not encouraged. Nancy and I wanted to have the rally there hoping to reach some of the young people from Howe.

The preacher who brought the message that night was not much more help with our goal than the singer was. When he first walked out on the football field, he grabbed the microphone and said, "Bless God, this is the first time I've set foot on one of these ungodly fields since God saved me."

After that outstanding opening statement, I heard many of the Howe students start their cars and watched them leave. Yes, the young people from the other AOG churches shouted and had a good time that night. But as far as the rally doing any good in reaching the young people in Howe, we didn't see any results from it.

As the church later began to grow in number, we sold the corner lot to First State Bank for $6,000.00. They got the land and allowed us to tear down the old building to use for lumber in our new church building. I used my front-end loader to push the building down, and then the real work began!

Most of the men of the church worked during the weekdays at their full-time jobs, but we didn't let that stop the work. Nancy headed up some of the women to pull nails and clean up the usable boards. My mother and dad drove over several times from Aubrey to Howe to help Nancy and her crew of mighty church women.

In addition to scrap wood from the old church building, a man in Sherman, Texas, gave us two old houses and one old building to tear down for the lumber. Sometimes, the men of the church were there to help, but most of the time, it was Nancy and her all-female work crew. In the end, most of the new church building was built out of the used lumber that the ladies had salvaged.

The team of mighty women of God didn't stop there. The brick that was used was also salvaged. It came from an old building in Van Alstyne that had been torn down. We paid for the brick and had to load, haul, and then unload the brick ourselves. Can you guess who helped load and unload those bricks? Nancy and her crew of faithful, God-loving church women! These are just some of the "works" recorded in God's Book of Records for Nancy and all the ladies of the church who worked so very hard.

During this whole process, I ripped some of the salvaged 2x12s into 2x4s (160 2x4s, each sixteen feet long) and had them stacked on the church's new concrete slab. On one Thursday night, while we were having a service in the Van Alstyne Nursing Home, someone stole every one of the 160 2x4s! There was a lot of sweat and hard labor involved with that lumber that was stolen that night. My sweet Nancy prayed that whatever they built with them would fall apart! Right or wrong, that's what she prayed.

The property purchased to build the new church building was on the south end of Howe on the west side of Highway 5, going toward Van Alstyne. We paid $3500.00 for the property, and it was low in some places (initially, about 50 percent of the property was in the flood plain). When it rained, water would stand five to six inches deep on most of it. But I had a 7-yard dump truck and a Massey Ferguson front-end loader, so I hauled in over four hundred loads of dirt to fill in the low places. (Actually, I stopped counting at the 400th load, so I really have no idea how many I hauled in after that.) I would dump the dirt, spread it out, and then drive over with the truck and front-end loader to compact the dirt. This went on for several weeks before the lot was ready for me to set the forms for the foundation of our new building.

We held the church services in our house until we had framed the front part of the new building. We built the Sunday School rooms, church office, and restrooms first. In the beginning, I purposefully left out one of the non-weight-bearing partitions that would eventually divide the room into Sunday School classrooms so that we would have one large room. That's where we met for church services until the main auditorium was completed.

I remember one Sunday morning that I sent my boys down to the railroad to gather enough rocks for everyone in the church to have one. I brought forth a message from John 8:7 about the woman caught in the act of adultery and Jesus saying let everyone without sin in their life cast the first stone. At the beginning of my message, I had the boys pass out the rocks. At the close of my message, I told them that the lesson is, "Let the one without any sin cast the first stone."

There was a young dad with his small son sitting in his lap right in front of me. His dad was letting him hold the rock, and—I bet you can guess already—the boy reared back and threw the stone, hitting me right above the right eye with that rock! I had a big goose egg on my forehead for the rest of that day. So much for that illustrative sermon! What could I say? Thank you, Jesus, for another educational experience.

I had planned to be pretty far along with the church building program before the winter of 1975 set in, so, in advance, I scheduled a revival with Brother JR Kneggs (who many called "Shoutin' Kneggs").[27] Unfortunately, when the date came around for him to come, we still had no heat (or air conditioning) in the front framed-in part of the new building where we were holding services.

I did have a kerosene blow heater, so we used that to warm the room up. However, we had to unplug it while Brother Kneggs was ministering because it was so loud that we couldn't hear anything the evangelist was saying with it running! Then, when the people's teeth began chattering from the cold, the evangelist would "pause for a good cause!" We would plug the heater back up and thaw the people out again, and on this went until he concluded the service.

Afterward, Brother Kneggs told Everett Mitchell, a building contractor in Sherman, Texas, about our situation concerning the heat and air. Mr. Mitchell donated a turnkey heat and air conditioning (HVAC) job for our new church building!

We sure had some fun times with all our children over the years, both in church and throughout their school years. One Sunday morning before church, one of the men, Brother Clint Krantz[28], came up to Anthony, our next to the oldest son. Brother Krantz asked Anthony, "Have you ever been licked?" Thinking he meant had he ever been "whipped" (beaten in a fight), Anthony bowed up and said, "No, sir!" Brother Krantz grabbed Anthony and quickly licked him on the side of his face and said, "Now you have been licked!" Anthony gagged, "Awe, man!" Anthony started wiping his face repeatedly. We got a good laugh out of that one.

One other afternoon, Shannon's teacher called Nancy to report on his shenanigans. It had rained very hard in a short period, and several streets in Sherman were flooding. Shannon's teacher had asked her students, "If the roads in Howe were flooding like the streets in Sherman, how would you be able to go home from school?" One by one, the students gave their answers. When it was Mister Shannon King's turn to respond, you won't guess what his answer was! He said he'd eat some beans and turn over on his back and putt-putt all the way home! (I don't know where he might have gotten his keen sense of humor from.)

Now, when it came to our daughter Renee, she would believe almost anything her daddy would tell her! For example, once, when I flipped the light switch to turn on the light, Renee asked me, "Daddy, how does flipping the switch make the light come on?" I told her that there were little bitty green men behind the switch plate, and when I flipped the switch, they would touch two wires together and make the light come on.

One morning, just as I was fixing to leave for work, Nancy said she was going to paint the walls in the kitchen. She asked me to remove the switch and wall plug (outlet) plates before I left. Just after I had removed the switch plate, Renee pulled up a kitchen chair to look at the open switch box. She turned around and said, "Daddy, I don't see any little green men in here." (And yes, in case you are wondering, her hair is kind of blonde.)

I recall when a particular family with six children started coming to church. Our son Anthony fell in love right away with the oldest daughter. The only thing wrong was the girl was much older and much taller than Anthony. But bless her heart, she would have pity for him. She'd sit low on the church pew so Anthony could sit high enough to put his arm around her. Sometimes, she would let him lay his head in her lap, and she would rub his precious little back. This is but one of the great memories of our children growing up on those old wooden church pews.

My mom and her three sisters all worked at the sewing factory[29] in Pilot Point for a season. At times, they would bring home some garments that were rejected for missing stitches and wouldn't pass inspection. The rejects were most often girls' and women's undergarments, so Mom and her sisters helped keep Nancy and Renee well-supplied with that kind of clothing. The only thing wrong with the garments is that, for some reason, the garments rejected in Renee's size were almost always in the color red! As a little girl, she did not want red underwear. She sometimes cried because all her little panties were red.

To help her overcome the disappointment, I would often encourage her when she ran out to greet me as I arrived home from work. I would reach down and pick her up and tell her not to cry, that I loved little girls who wore red panties. Innocently, as her father, I thought that this would make her feel good about wearing her (free) red panties and so she would not cry. As you might guess, that little innocent encouragement of my daughter got me in big trouble without me even knowing that I was in trouble or why!

On one Sunday night, as usual, I was to lead the song service. Our piano player would always look at me to tell her the page number of the song. This Sunday night, she would not even look at me. With each song, she continued to avert her eyes away from me, and I really began to wonder, "What on earth is wrong?" I pondered what I had possibly said or done so that she wouldn't even look at me. After the service, I was worried about it. I was telling Nancy, and she grinned and said, "I bet I know why!"

Nancy said that when the pianist was coming inside the church that evening, Renee had run up to her and asked her what color her panties were! She whispered to Renee in a hushed reply that they were red. Evidently, then Renee grinned widely and said, "Boy, my daddy will really like you!"

Our son Nathanael wasn't without his share of cute stories, either. But he was born several years after this, so those are included in later chapters. But while we were in Howe, we had some good times, some embarrassing times, and yes, we had some very rough times.

In many of the tough times, I came home so tired from working on the job, yet still, I needed to work on the church building. In addition, I needed to spend time in prayer, study, and preach three times a week. I would get so discouraged at times. In those times, my sweet, faith-filled Nancy would encourage me not to give up. She would tell me to keep on trusting God, for He would give me the strength to carry on. I would never have made it without God and Nancy's helping hands and precious heart.

Even still, with all the roadblocks that Satan placed in front of us, the church was able to reach outside its walls and minister in different ways in many other places. Every Thursday night, we held a service at a Nursing Home in Van Alstyne. On many Sunday afternoons, I would go to the Grayson County Jail and preach to the inmates there. We had a deputy sheriff who attended our church and would often bring inmates to our Sunday morning services. We were thankful to be reaching our community as well as the surrounding communities.

Our church received very little support in the form of money from the Denton Section (although they did offer me a lot of super holy advice). The banks, when considering loaning to a church, looked at the number of members and how much money the church brought in annually before they'd consider loaning money to a church. Well, our small church didn't qualify for a church loan.

In the end, Nancy and I personally borrowed $10,000.00. Nancy's station wagon (that was all paid for), my pickup (also entirely debt-free), the custom-made trailer that I used to haul my tractor, and my dump truck were all put up for security on the loan. It was a one-year demand note. The banker I borrowed the money from told me if I was unable to pay the note off on the due date, he would let me pay the interest and renew the note for another year.

When the note was due, it was wintertime. We had snow and ice all over the ground. I had three houses to build, and I had all three foundations set up and ready to pour the concrete. The weather was so bad I couldn't pour the foundations until the properties dried up where I could clean up all the mud that had washed into the beams so they would pass inspection for us to pour.

I was counting on having those foundations poured and making a financial draw on the work completed on those projects. Then, I would have enough money in hand so that Nancy and I could pay the bank note off and release our assets from security on the loan. However, no completed foundations meant no draws, and that meant no money.

Although I didn't have what we needed to pay off the note, I did have enough money put back to pay the interest, so I stopped by the bank. Much to my surprise, I found out that the man who had made me the loan was no longer available. The man I initially dealt with in taking out the loan and his brother were the largest lenders in the bank at the time. But evidently, he had a drinking problem. During the year that passed, the bank board of examiners removed him from dealing with the public and assigned all the loan cases to other loan officers.

I met the new man that I was to deal with. He asked if I was able to pay the entire note in full. Of course, I answered, "No." I told him what the other man who gave me the loan had assured me. The new representative informed me that I would now deal with him and him alone. I was prepared to pay the interest and request an extension for another year. So, I offered to pay the interest, but he refused to take it. He yelled at me that it was a demand note and he was demanding payment in full or the bank would immediately start the foreclosure process. And that's exactly what happened.

The borrowed funds had already been invested in the church building project. Because the loan was personally secured by Nancy and me, when the bank foreclosed on the loan, Nancy and I were left without any transportation. She had no family vehicle to transport the children or run errands; I had no truck, no tractor, no dump truck. We had to call on Nancy's dad for help, who brought over a car for us to drive until I could figure out other arrangements.

We put everything on the line to build that church building, and help from the district or section boards was nowhere to be found. On top of that, after the Howe State Bank sold off our vehicles for a small amount of money, they also got a judgment against us personally for the balance of the note plus 9 percent interest until paid in full. And we still had no means to pay any more than we had before. We were all but ruined financially. We gave our all to the reopening of that church, and it cost our family everything. We had no way to recover.

I drove over to the Pilot Point National Bank and explained our situation to the banker there. Kindly, he listened to every word I said, and then he eyed me up and down for some time. He had known me nearly all my life. Finally, he asked me to go to a specific used car dealer in Denton. He instructed Nancy to pick out a used car and for me to pick out a used pickup. We were to tell the used car salesperson to call him at the bank to make payment arrangements. Yes, God will make a way when there seems to be no way!

God had rescued us with provision for transportation, and we were so grateful. At the same time, I felt so let down that the Denton Section nor the North Texas District offered any help. After all, the borrowed monies were all spent on the church building, which was deeded to the Denton Section and North Texas District of the Assemblies of God. They had the property and the title deed, and we had the debt. It didn't seem right.

After that intensely stressful and disappointing ordeal, Nancy and I resigned from the First Assembly of God in Howe and moved back to a rented house in Aubrey, Texas. In spite of the tragedy it caused for our family, our precious seed in that church survived as Rev. Billy Mills pastored until August of 1980, and during this time, he framed the current sanctuary. After him, Rev. Sam Nuckels pastored the church from 1980 to 1982, and during this time, he completed the construction of the building.[30]

We weren't there for the building's completion, but our hearts, the work of our hands (and many others), and sacrificial giving by our entire family laid the foundation of that church in Howe. The Church and the building still stand to this date as a part of our legacy. It was later renamed New Beginning Fellowship (2010) and, most recently, Summit View Church (2021).[31]

Starting over and hoping for a fresh start, we quickly found that the impact of that disappointing season was not over. The good news was that I had passed my ordination exam and was standing on the stage with the other Ordination Candidates at the District Council that year, waiting to be anointed, ordained, and prayed over by the

District Officials. But, in the midst of what should be a cause for celebration, the District Superintendent pulled me out of the lineup. He broke the news to me that the Presbyter of the Denton Section had reported that I had left Howe owing the uncollected debt, and he wouldn't approve my application for ordination!

Thankfully, I had an advocate in the District Superintendent who had pulled me out of the lineup that night. The Superintendent said that if he were me, he'd move out of the Denton Section as soon as possible. He recommended that I check with the Arkansas District to see if any churches were open in the state of Arkansas. He said it was a good district to be in and that he would personally see that Nancy and I would have a good recommendation from the North Texas District. So, we followed the advice of the North Texas District Superintendent!

In the latter part of 1978, Nancy and I called the Arkansas District to see what churches may be open and needing a pastor. The Arkansas District let us know of several churches looking for pastors at that time. We began to pray for God's will to be done and for God to guide us to the right one. Our little family was soon on the move once again.

Chapter Five

We gave much thought and prayer to the list of churches that the Arkansas District had given us. When we both had peace about a selection, we called the Roseville Assembly of God in Roseville, Arkansas, who agreed to schedule us for a weekend to come and preach.

As we prepared for the weekend, I remembered something related to our journey to Arkansas. This happened long before Nancy and I married, in my childhood, living at home with my parents. Every time things were not going in a manner pleasing to my dad, or life was unfolding in a way that didn't quite suit him, he would always say he was going to sell out and move all of us to Arkansas! Guess what? He never did. As a result, I thought I might never get to live in Arkansas, known as "the land of opportunity." But isn't it just like God to see fit and make the way for Nancy and me to live in Arkansas with our young family? At least for a short time, it was our land of opportunity!

We arrived with all the children in tow, preached on the scheduled Sunday, and the vote was held at the following midweek service. All but two people voted us in, and the Roseville Assembly of God confirmed us as their new pastors. I was 36 years old, Nancy was 29 years old, Shannon was 13, Anthony was 11, and Renee was 9 years old when we moved to Arkansas for new opportunities.

On our first official Sunday as pastor at the Roseville church, we pulled up and parked. Right about that same time, a pickup truck pulled up and parked beside us. As I was getting out of our car, a lady from the pickup walked up to me and introduced herself. Then she introduced her

ROSEVILLE ASSEMBLY OF GOD, ROSEVILLE, AR[36]

husband, who had walked up and stood beside her. She said that she and her husband were the ones who voted against us. She didn't think I was big enough to pastor the church. She said she was telling me this so that Nancy and I wouldn't have to sneak around and try to find out who it was that voted against us. Not discouraged, I called her by her name and said that a time would come for Nancy and me to leave and no longer pastor the Roseville church. I was confident that by that time, she and I would be the best of friends. She quickly answered that she doubted that would happen, but I knew it would be true!

As that first Sunday morning service began, everything seemed to be moving along well. That is… until I started to preach! During my message, an older man came up front and said he was having chest pains and wanted me to anoint and pray for him. I started looking inside the pulpit for the olive oil to anoint the man and couldn't see it anywhere. Finally, one of the men in the church came up on the platform and found it in another small cabinet. I anointed the forehead of the elderly man with chest pain and closed my eyes to begin to pray.

Suddenly, there was a loud boom, and some of the people started to loudly scream. I quickly opened my eyes and saw that one of the enormous light globes had fallen and hit a teenage boy on the top of his head, shattering all over the place. The wife of the elderly man who had asked for prayer jumped up and exclaimed that this was all an omen from God, signaling that this Texas preacher should not be here! (At that point, I was inclined to agree.) Her husband yelled back at her and said, "Shut up, Mammie. You ain't right in the head anyhow. It's just that a light globe was loose and fell and whacked Buddy Black on the head. Get the wackuum (vacuum) cleaner and wackuum all this mess up!"

Later, we learned that the elder's wife had previously had rheumatic fever, and it had somewhat affected her mind. We also discovered that he was a preacher and had at one time pastored the Roseville church. Another coincidence we found was that their last name was also King, but we were never able to find any connection or kinship with our family.

Brother King was instrumental in helping me to learn where the families of the church lived, including those who used to attend the church. He would also take me on tours of a lot of off-road areas and trails.

On one such trip, we came upon a running creek with just a low-water crossing. The water was crystal clear and looked about a foot deep to me. I asked him if they always just drove through it, and he answered, "Yes." So, I drove into the stream of water. Midstream, my pickup drowned out, and water slowly began to fill the inside of it. In fact, it filled up knee-high as we sat there in the seat of my truck! I turned and looked at him and said, "I thought you said that you drove through it all the time!" He laughed and called me a dumb Texas driver and said, "We don't drive through it when the water is this high." Good thing for us, or perhaps it was a God thing, a school bus came along and pushed us on through to the other side of the creek. (You know they wouldn't do that nowadays!)

There are a series of locks and dams on the Arkansas River. We had one near us in the town of Ozark. I like to watch them raise and lower the water levels for the barges coming up and downstream. It was an interesting process to observe; at least, it was for me.

Our family lived in the church parsonage located about a half mile from the Roseville church. The church was located about a quarter of a mile from the Arkansas River. The river had a left-hand bend in it that was almost directly behind the church. When tugboats pushed barges down the river, the huge engines would literally vibrate the church pews! Those same massive engines would also vibrate the beds in the parsonage at night, which took quite some time for us all to get used to!

Aside from the tugboat engine vibrations, there were advantages to living so close to the river. Sometimes, I would sneak down to one of the small creeks that flowed into the Arkansas River. I liked to lie down in the high grass to watch a den of beavers at work. I noticed that there would always be one designated beaver who would act as a lookout to warn the other workers of any approaching danger. When the lookout beaver would slap its tail several times in the water as an alert, the worker beavers quickly disappeared. When the lookout decided that the coast was clear, it would slap its tail in the water again. At the all-clear, the workers appeared and were "busy as beavers" once again!

Many afternoons, Nancy and I would drive the country roads so she could see the deer. She loved just watching the deer out in the open fields or wooded areas. She always enjoyed the simple things in life—I guess that's why she put up with me for so many years. (You can grin and keep your thoughts to yourself on that.)

It was in front of the Roseville Assembly of God that Nancy heard the audible voice of God speak to her. On that day, some of the young people had planned to go somewhere after the Sunday morning service. They wanted our eldest son to go with them to do whatever they had planned to do that afternoon; the front seat of the truck was already full of other kids, but Shannon had been invited to go along if he didn't mind riding in the back of the pickup (which was common back then). Nancy was just fixing to say that he could go when she heard the voice of God tell her, "No!" So, she did not give him permission to go. It turned out to be a life-saving step of obedience to the voice of God.

We received news later that the driver of the pickup lost control of the vehicle, and the truck ran off the road, crashing into a huge tree not far from the church. The ones who were in the accident suffered severe head injuries. It was sobering to realize that had Shannon been with them, he could have also been severely injured or worse. It was a strong lesson in learning to heed the voice of God!

The Roseville parsonage had a five-acre pasture on one side, and Sugar Hill Farms was on the other side of our place. Two families that attended the Roseville church lived and worked on the Sugar Hill Farms.[32] Quite often, the families who worked on the farm next to us would call and ask if we wanted to ride horses up on Tanyard Mountain, which was part of the Sugar Hill Farms land. The families always had enough horses and saddles so that all of us could take and enjoy the horseback rides. Most of the time, we would happily meet up with them and be excited to enjoy the ride.

Often, I would have to catch and saddle the horse I was going to ride, but every now and then, the farm hands would already have the horses caught and saddled up, ready for me to ride. I quickly learned that when that was the case, the horse would be what was called "green broke." This meant we'd have a bucking ride for a little while!

I decided that I rather enjoyed those rides, and I knew we had room for a horse in the five-acre pasture next to the house. So, very much against Sister Nancy's wishes, Brother Gene (me) bought a bucking horse! I had him delivered to the small pasture next to our house. I saddled him up and attempted to ride him, not once but eight times, before I was too sore and bruised to get back on.

Around that time, there was a country western song called "The Strawberry Roan." It had been around for a while but was sung most famously during our era by Marty Robbins. It's about a bucking horse that would get all wound up and buck hard and high. The lyrics include a portion that says, "He's about the worst bucker I've seen on the range, he'll turn on a nickel and give you some change... I'll bet all my money, the man ain't alive that'll stay with Old Strawberry when he makes his high dive."[33]

After my eighth try on my new ride, I looked over to see my sweet bride standing at the gate singing the song "Strawberry Roan" to me! And, when I looked toward the County Road that ran in front of the house, I saw several of the church people sitting on the tailgates of their pickups, laughing at the show I had put on for them! After some time, I was able to ride Ole' Bucky. However, any time he was of a mind to, he'd still throw whoever was on his back—my younger brother Gaylon will vouch for that!

One very hot Texas afternoon, I saddled up ole' Bucky. He and I made our way down to Sugar Hill Farms' shop building, which was a little over a quarter of a mile from our house. By the time we arrived, I was hot and thirsty, so I went over to an outside faucet. It had a long garden hose rolled up and hooked up to it. As I turned the faucet on, the water began to run out of the hose, but it was all milky-colored. I let it run for a little while before I started drinking from it. As I began to swallow the water, my mouth and throat began to burn, and my stomach began to burn like it was on fire!

Right about then, the Jackson brothers, who worked there, saw me and asked if I got a drink from the garden hose. Of course, I said, "Yes!" And they told me they had just gotten through using the hose to spray the whole herd of cattle with tick poison! Feeling sick all over, I got back on ole' Bucky and headed home as fast as I could.

I began to pray and quote the Scripture over and over where Jesus said if we drank any deadly thing, it should not harm us! By the time I reached the house, my whole inside was burning like fire. One of my boys put Bucky back in the pasture for me. Our back porch had several steps that I had to climb to get inside the house, and I was in no shape to make it up those steps. Looking outside, Nancy saw that something was wrong with me. She rushed out to help me up the steps and into the house.

I began to explain to her what had happened to me, and she immediately called the Poison Control Center in Little Rock, Arkansas. The first question they asked was what kind of chemical poison it was. Nancy hung up and called the Sugar Hill Farms shop building to ask what type of poison they had used to spray the cows with. They hurried and brought one of the empty containers up to our house. Nancy called Little Rock again to tell them the name of the product. They replied that I must have run more water through the hose than I thought I had, or I would already be dead! Little Rock Poison Control called in a prescription at the Paris Drug Store, which was eight miles away from us. They said it would empty my stomach, and believe you me, that it did—from both ends. I believe the healing hand of God was riding ole' Bucky with me that day, or I would have never made it. I kept ole'

Bucky the whole time we were there, and when I moved back to Texas, I moved him too.

The Roseville church's collections of tithe and offerings were never enough to support us full-time. I worked at several part-time jobs. I swept floors at a feed mill in Paris, Arkansas. I worked at a groundhog sawmill, pulling slabs and stacking lumber. I helped a house framing crew when they needed extra help. I always said that I would work to preach, but I wouldn't quit preaching to work.

Late one afternoon, I got a call from the man who owned and ran the sawmill. (It was called a "groundhog sawmill" because of the sawdust left after the cutting. Basically, it is a portable circle mill run by a diesel engine to cut logs from small tracts of land. Once you are done cutting, there is nothing left but a pile of sawdust, similar to a groundhog burrow.) The owner asked me to come and help him for a day or two. He said he needed help to cut a truckload of lumber. He stated that he needed to cut and sell the lumber to the lumber yard so that he could pay some overdue bills. I agreed to help him and arrived bright and early the following day, ready to work.

Right off the bat, our workday got interesting! The sawmill man tried to crank and start the engine that ran the sawmill, but it would not start. The sawmill owner called and told his wife to bring olive oil, anoint the machinery, and pray for the engine to start. His wife walked up from their house to the sawmill, puffing away on a long cigarette. She spoke to me first, and then she laid her cigarette down on a flat rock. I watched her take the olive oil bottle and splash some oil on the engine's hood. She then laid her hand on the hood of the engine and began to pray:

Oh Lord, you know my husband is lazy and won't work unless we have a bunch of overdue bills to pay. Well, Lord, we've got some bills that need to be paid, and we need this engine to start and run so my husband and Brother King can saw enough lumber to pay the bills we owe. Thank you, Lord, for answering my prayer in advance. Amen.

She then smiled and told her husband to turn the crank. He winked at me and said, "Watch this!" He just barely turned the crank, and the engine started purring. His wife picked up her cigarette from the rock, and off she went toward home, puffing away.

But that was not the end of the story that day. As he pulled the lever to engage the clutch that kicked in to start the big saw-blade turning, some of the replaceable teeth flew off the big blade. We looked around to find the teeth that flew off, but our efforts were in vain. We couldn't find them. The sawmill owner asked me if I had any money that he could borrow from me to run to town and buy some new teeth for the big blade. I had to tell him I was just as broke as he was. So, he called his wife again and told her to come back… and bring the olive oil with her!

I was kind of impressed with her praying for the engine to start, but I did not have faith for her to pray for the miracle to happen with the missing teeth from the saw-blade! I began to doubt like doubting Thomas with this one. Nonetheless, his wife came back up the hill with another cigarette, puffing away, with the bottle of olive oil in her hand. She laid her cigarette down on the same flat rock. After her husband explained the situation of missing teeth to her, she walked over, anointed the big ole saw-blade, and looked up to pray—it was nearly the same prayer that she had prayed when she prayed for the engine to start. She looked at her husband, smiled, and said, "Start her up and saw away!"

As I said, I didn't have faith that this saw-blade was going to cut through the size logs we had to process that day. But guess what? It cut through the logs just like cutting hot butter! His wife picked up her cigarette and headed back down the hill, puffing away.

When I got home, I told Nancy that I was never going to preach against smoking ever again! Nancy asked me why, and I explained the events of the day and how the woman was so confident that God was going to answer her prayer. And God did answer her prayers that day, both times. Now, I am not promoting the use of tobacco products, but I will say it didn't hinder her praying or God's answering one bit! I witnessed God answering her prayers, so I would have to admit that it was definitely her faith, not mine, that God honored that day.

My sweet Nancy was like that woman of prayer, well, without the cigarettes! Nancy was a woman of prayer who prayed not only over the big things but also over the small things. For example, when pennies, nickles, and dimes were few and far between, Nancy prayed that God would lead her to the right garage sales where she would find the exact size of clothing needed for our children. Nancy was skilled at being led by God and how to make every cent stretch as far as was required.

Our first three children were spaced two years apart. When they were small, Nancy took all three with her any time she went grocery shopping, to the washateria (laundromat), or to take care of any household errands or business. Very seldom did she ever leave her babies with someone else to babysit them so she could have time to herself. Nancy cleaned her house, her mother's house, and the house of a sister-in-law who was sick and unable to keep her house clean. Always ready to help anyone in need, she would pick up other children walking to and from school on cold days. Nancy even found a way to purchase coats, socks, and shoes for some of them. On occasion, she bought eyeglasses, school supplies, and other necessities for several children. Only a few of our closest friends knew about these acts of sacrificial generosity.

I remember one time, however, she was able to buy something new for all our kids from the store. Anthony couldn't believe that his pants were brand new! He questioned her over and over to be sure he was hearing her right that nobody had ever worn them before. Shannon was so proud of his new pants that he stood up and wouldn't sit in the back seat of the car because he didn't want to wrinkle his new pants. Nancy always put herself last when it came to buying clothes. Oh! If only she could have realized her own actual value and worth in this old world.

One year, however, when Nancy and I were making plans to attend the District Council (in Texas), I was finally able to talk her into buying herself a new dress. She shopped around and picked out one that she liked that was within her price range. When we got to the first service, another preacher's wife came over, and she was wearing a dress that looked just like Nancy's. The only difference in the dresses was the stores in which they were purchased. Apparently, the other lady purchased hers in an upscale shop and paid somewhat more for her dress than Nancy did for hers (and might have been proud of that). The other lady asked Nancy where she got the money to buy her dress, saying that she didn't know that Nancy had ever shopped at the store from which she had bought her dress. Nancy smiled and said, "God provides in mysterious ways." As for me, I had to pray through because I wanted to tell that lady what cliff she could fall from.

God blessed the church, and the congregation began to grow in numbers. Several who had left the church started coming back to worship with us. But who else knows that often, when God starts to move, the old devil fights harder than ever to cause distractions? One such distraction occurred on a Sunday night as I had just opened my Bible.

As I began to read my Scripture text, we heard loud gunshots right in front of the church. A young teenage boy jumped up and ran out of the church to see what was going on while all the adult men of the church just sat there. I was so worried about the safety of the young boy that I closed my Bible and walked outside to see what was happening. I saw a young man standing in the church's parking lot with a pistol in his hand. I had already met him a short time before and knew that he was married to a lady whose parents lived next door to the church.

I called him by name and asked him what was going on. He replied that his wife had left him and gone back to her parents' house. He was trying to put a little fright into her to make her come back home. I assured him his chances of her coming back would be much better if he'd stop shooting at her parents' house!

The following morning, the young man drove up to the parsonage and tried to give me a bottle of whiskey and a six-pack of beer. I said, "No, thank you. I don't drink alcohol." He smiled and said, "Come on, Rev, all preachers do; they just don't want the people of their church to know they do." That may be true of some, but not this preacher. I chalked this up to another educational experience while pastoring!

At one point in Roseville, we hosted a revival with Evangelist Bob Teel. He and his wife, Jan, are both ordained with the Oklahoma District Council of the Assemblies of God.

On one of the revival nights, I set a fifty-five-gallon barrel in the middle of the church's parking lot so that we could have a "hallelujah bonfire." Several young people and even some adults brought their heavy metal rock music albums and threw them into the barrel. We poured some gas on them and lit them on fire. Demons thrive on that kind of music, but not everyone understands that or gets revived in a revival! Some people (who missed out on the bonfire night) were mad because we burned the records before giving them the opportunity to see if there were any of them that they might have wanted to take home!

Late one Sunday night, Nancy and I received a phone call after we had already gone to bed. A mother and dad were crying, praying, and begging us to come and help them pray with their teenage daughter. They said a demon had control of her and was speaking through her. We hurried as fast as we could to get all our own children out of bed and dressed. When we arrived at their house, the girl was sitting in a chair. The first thing I did was place my Bible on top of her head while Nancy, her parents, and I all began to pray. I said, "devil, you cannot withstand the Word of God."

We all began to plead the Blood of Jesus over the girl. The demonic voice speaking through the girl would tell me that it hated me. I remembered Brother M. R. Russell telling me that if you could get the person to say the name of Jesus, the demons would come out of them. Demons fear and tremble at just the mention of His name, Jesus. When the girl would try to say, "Jesus." The old devil would choke her all up. But finally, she spoke the name of Jesus, and you could literally feel the evil presence of the demons leave her body! The girl went limp and nearly fell out of the chair. Nancy opened the door to the outside and said, "devil, you get out of here right now!"

The girl stood up and hugged my neck, saying, "Brother King, I don't hate you. I love you and Sister King!" Then, she shared with us how she arrived at that night's experience. She said she would be in her bedroom, listening to an album by the heavy metal rock band called KISS, with her strobe light flashing. She said that was when the demon(s) would come up to the window. Before long, she said they weren't just outside the window but came into the room with her and entered her body. As I said, demons thrive in that kind of music, and it's sad to say that it is still found even in some churches today.

There was rarely a dull time while we were in Roseville. Early one morning, a man called me and asked me if I wanted a "horg" (hog). I thought it was already butchered, so I answered, "Sure!"

In a little while, the man pulled up in a pickup truck with a live hog in the back of the truck bed! I quickly realized that I had no pen to put the hog in, but I didn't want him to get the best of me in the situation. So, I had the bright idea to tie some electrical wire to one of the pig's hind legs and tie the other end of the electrical wire to a tree in our front yard. I thanked him for the hog, and he went on his way.

News travels fast in rural areas, just in case you didn't know. It wasn't long before I noticed several of the church people driving by, looking at the pig tied to the tree. My sweet Nancy had her two cents worth to put in on the situation going on in our front yard. She told me I was acting like I was raised in Arkansas instead of Texas! Ouch! No offense to our Arkansas folks, but that got this Texas man moving and before the day ended, the boys and I built a hog pen for Mr. Piggy!

As Mr. Piggy grew, I was looking forward to all the provisions he would bring to our meals! Unfortunately, my sweet Nancy fell in love with him. So, guess what? We didn't get to eat any of Mr. Piggy. That big ole' hog became a family pet until we headed back to Texas! When we did finally move away, we took him to another local family. They most likely had many good meals from that hog after we left.

The small community of Roseville was about eight miles from Ozark, Arkansas, on a curvy stretch of road. One day, Nancy was driving some of the church's young people to see something over in the town of Ozark. She said she took some of the curves a little faster than usual, and a young person asked if Sister Nancy had been a race-car driver before she became a preacher's wife. She laughed about it as she was telling me. (Really, though, her driving scared me most of the time too!)

Arkansas is a beautiful state, and our family enjoyed living there. We still visit some of the church folks from time to time when we are in that vicinity. One fond memory is of a wintry Saturday when we had an unusually heavy snowstorm. A large group from the church decided to meet up at Cove Lake for some wintertime fun.

Donald and Lola Corley (of Ozark) were among our church friends at the lake that day. Nancy and Lola Corley were watching the kids from both families playing in the snow not far off from where Don Corley and I were standing. Don told me to tell them to come and stand under the beautiful snow-covered tree with us. So, I called Nancy and Lola over. Little did I know that Don was going to kick the trunk of the tree, causing great loads of snow to rain down on top of us all, covering us from head to toe! Nancy never believed me when I said I really did not know what Don Corley was up to until he actually kicked the tree. Another family had brought an old car hood and rope, which we hooked up behind a pickup like a giant sled. The grownups and kids alike all had great fun that snowy winter day.

When our term was up serving in the pastorate at Roseville, the church voted to extend another term to us. (The vote was not 100%, but I believe there were only four or five who voted no to extending another term.)

After much prayer, we decided not to accept another term because it so happened that my sweet Nancy was pregnant. The baby was due on the 14th or 15th of February, 1980, but Nancy was having some health problems with her pregnancy. We felt it was time to return to Pilot Point, Texas, to be closer to the doctors and hospital in Denton.

As we were loading the U-haul truck, I have to tell you that the lady who, on our first day in Roseville, was confident we would not be friends, stood in our driveway, crying and begging us to stay! We cherished our times together and all that God had accomplished. Still, Nancy and I knew in our hearts that we needed to head out for Pilot Point, nearer to the hospital in Denton. We were ever so glad we made that decision!

After arriving in Texas, we found out that Nancy had toxemia, and her blood pressure was sky-high. The doctor was afraid we were going to lose her and the baby. They had to do an emergency cesarean section surgery to deliver the baby, who arrived on January 8, 1980, thirty-eight days early.

Nathan (Nathanael) only weighed four and a half pounds at birth. I could lay his little head in the palm of my right hand, and his little feet barely reached the bend of my elbow. The hospital kept him in the pediatric ward for two weeks with constant care. Nancy and I had to suit up to visit and hold the baby.

Nancy was dismissed from the hospital in four days, but she had to come back and breastfeed the baby every day he remained in the hospital. Being under the oxygen tank for so long when he was born did have some effect on his eyesight, so he has worn glasses or contact lenses nearly all his life.

Nevertheless, Nathanael grew up to be a strong, intelligent young man. Now that he is fully grown, he's not quite as tall as his two older brothers, but he says, "It's OK because it's in the *'Gene's'.*" I guess he means it wasn't caused by his early arrival but that he's just short, like me. (I told you he wasn't without his share of humor and cute stories!)

When he was little, he would go upstairs to our bedroom and ask Nancy all sorts of questions about George Washington's mother! We couldn't figure out why he was so fixed on questions about Washington's mother, but he was! Finally, Nancy told him she never knew Mrs. Washington, George's mother, and Anthony needed to quit worrying so much about George Washington's mother, get back in his bed, and go to sleep!

At other times, if our bedroom door was shut, Nathan would come and stick his little fingers under the door and ask his mother if she could see his fingers. When she would tell him she could see them, he would start singing the song by Ricky Skaggs, "Honey (Open the door.)"

> Honey... Honey... Honey, won't you open that door? This is your sweet daddy; don't you love me no more? It's cold outside; let me sleep on the floor. Honey, won't you open that door?[34]

Chapter Six

While living in Pilot Point, I got a job in Dallas working for a drywall company. Nancy's mother lived just six miles from us and was a great help with caring for the children (and Nancy) during Nancy's recovery. As Nancy and the newborn baby began to grow stronger each day, I began to pray and ask God to show us His will for our family's future. I started to make calls concerning open churches needing pastors.

It was early in 1980 that we tried out for the First Assembly of God in Azle, Texas. We missed being voted in as pastors by only two votes. Afterward, over five of the families who were attending the First Assembly of God in Azle contacted us to pray about moving to Azle and starting a new church.

I contacted the North Fort Worth section and asked their permission to start the new church as an Assemblies of God church. They refused to grant us permission to start another AOG church in the Azle area. So, with their refusal, I turned in my Assemblies of God minister's license so that we could pastor the new congregation of people anyway. We made the move to Azle and started having church in the home of one of those families.

We eventually rented a metal building to have church in, and we named the church Calvary Assembly—note that we left off the "of God" part of the name. It wasn't long until I began to realize that some of the people who had come over to the new church might just have been the thorn in the flesh at the previous one. It soon became apparent that we may have actually done the First Assembly of God in Azle a big favor.

After a few months, the North Texas District Superintendent called and asked us to pray about trying out for the Gunter Assembly of God in Alba, Texas. He said that every time he prayed concerning the church in Alba, my face would appear before him. I called his attention to the fact that I no longer had papers with the North Texas district. He assured me that if the people voted me in, the district would see that I had my papers back.

After much prayer, Nancy and I felt led to contact the church in Alba. They already had a name or two, but the deacon we contacted said the board would pray for God's guidance. The next day, they called and scheduled us to come try out the following weekend. We preached the Sunday morning service and preached the Sunday night service. They voted right after the Sunday night service ended. The vote was 100 percent for receiving us as pastors. The former pastor and his wife were there when they voted. He had pastored the church for over thirty years. He congratulated us and offered to be of help in any way he could. He also promised to help and not hinder us in any way as the church's new pastors. He proved to be a man of his word to Nancy and me.

In the early part of 1981, about a year after moving to Azle, we moved to Alba to pastor the Gunter Assembly of God. I was 38, Nancy was 31, Shannon was 15, Anthony was 13, Renee was 11, and Nathan was nearly one year old. The parsonage was next door to the church. The congregation was made up of young and old alike; I'd say about half and half. We immediately noticed that there was a calm, sweet spirit in the church, and they were an

GUNTER ASSEMBLY OF GOD, ALBA, TX

easy congregation to preach to. Nathanael, being a baby who was not quite a year old, was quickly a favorite. Sister Ragsdale started calling him *Shug*, which was short for sugar. The older women of the church always wanted to hold him and soon had him spoiled rotten.

The Gunter church in Alba had four deacons. These were good men who loved God and wanted God's will to be done within the church in all its activities. But there was one problem that I noticed right away. One of these deacons was nearly always late for church. This same man was known to talk out loud during church, too. He would sit in the back of the church and start passing out chewing gum to all the young people. The commotion from all that would usually calm down in just a little bit unless, of course, he ran out of gum before all the young people got some. Then we had a real problem! You couldn't help but like that deacon, though, for he was still a kid at heart, living in a grown man's body. He was a tender-hearted man who was always willing to lend a helping hand to anyone who needed help. Once, he told me to go fill up our car with gas at the local station and charge it to his account. He said each month, he paid tickets charged to him by people he didn't even know!

This same deacon ran a dairy farm and farmed several acres of farmland where he always had a big watermelon crop. Some of the deacon's family members would help sell the melons. Besides the sales by family members, there was a big old tree by the roadside just before you entered the city of Emory, Texas. The deacon would leave his big watermelons under the shade of the tree with an "honor system" money jar for folks to leave their payment for the melons in. He said he never had a melon taken without the money being in the money jar. Years later, after Nancy and I had left the church, we came back to preach at the church's homecoming (anniversary) service. On our way home, we passed that same tree. There in the shade were his watermelons and the money jar. I stopped and picked up two big melons and started to put an IOU note in the money jar. Nancy saw what I was doing, and she took out my IOU and replaced it with money in the jar for the melons so that the deacon would still never have a melon taken without money being put in the jar!

One of the four deacons was a Drywaller. Sometimes, I would help with drywall for extra money. Another one of the deacons installed septic tanks, and I would, from time to time, do that as well to earn extra cash. I was always picking up extra work to supplement our income because the churches we pastored rarely paid us enough to support our family. But God was faithful, and Nancy was good at making every bit cover what we needed.

One of our regular church members, Charles Knapp, owned and ran a dairy farm. Their farm was just a short distance from our house. Anthony was 13 years old at the time, and sometimes, I'd let him drive my pickup down to their dairy farm. He worked and did odd jobs for the brother and sister at the dairy farm.

This dairy farmer's wife's first name was Ineda, and her last name was Knapp. Yes. That's right. Ineda Knapp. She was one of the church's greeters. Every time she would introduce herself to visitors, she'd have to explain that Ineda Knapp (sounds like "I need a nap") was her real name.

One Sunday night, I was walking across the church's parking lot from the church parsonage next door. A car turned in too short, missed the culvert, and blew out a tire. I walked quickly over to see if anyone was hurt, and a young man got out of the car. He told me that God had turned his car in the direction of the church's parking lot. I grinned and said to him that if God had turned his car, he would not have missed the driveway! I invited the young man to stay for church that night, and he agreed to stay.

When the altar call was given, the young man came and knelt to pray. An elderly lady who always sat on the front pew with her walking stick began to pray with the young man at the altar. Every time the young man would try to get up, she would hit him with her cane and make him kneel back down and keep on praying. After several times, I finally walked over and told her to let him get up. When he finally got up, I asked him if you felt any different, and he said yes, that his leg tingled. He had knelt so long that his leg had gone to sleep while he was kneeling to pray.

I don't know about other preachers, but the way the Holy Spirit starts to build a message within me is that it usually begins with a Scripture coming to mind. Then, as I think about that Scripture passage, additional thoughts start to pop into my mind. That is how the messages that I preach begin to come together. I usually start praying and seeking God for my Sunday morning messages on Thursday mornings. One week in particular, Thursday morning came and passed with no scripture and no thoughts coming up in my heart as I prayed. Friday came and went and still no scripture or thoughts. Saturday, the same thing happened. Sunday morning, I went over to the church early, and I began to pray. Sunday school started and ended, and I was still in the church office praying with no message to preach. The song service started and ended, and I walked up to the pulpit.

I was going to tell the people that I was sorry, but I had no message to preach that day. Just then, one of the older men jumped up and began to testify! The man was an old bachelor who never had a whole lot to say, but he had a lot to say this time. While he was testifying, the Spirit of God began to move throughout the congregation. Young and old alike filled the altars. I learned a lot that Sunday morning. I found out that I don't have to preach every service. But praying and seeking God for His will to be done is necessary regardless.

This church furnished the parsonage for us to live in, but even with that, our weekly salary was not enough to support a family of six. I often worked odd jobs to keep things going, even driving from Alba to Dallas to find work. Does that sound familiar? We had been through that situation before! But do you remember the story early in the book about the professional gambler in the first church we pastored? The one in Whitewright? Well (as luck and/or the Lord would have it), when we moved to the Gunter church, we discovered we once again had a connection with a (different) professional gambler in the church!

The wife and son in this family (whose father was a gambler) started coming to church on a regular basis. The gambling man came to service the day we baptized his wife and son. After that, like the other gambler in the Whitewright church, this man would periodically send a large sum of money with his wife to pay tithes from his winnings. Since offerings in this church (also much like the Whitewright church) were usually very limited—right or wrong—Nancy and I often prayed for him to win!

Another significant memory from our time at Gunter Assembly of God actually started with an encounter way back in 1966. During the time that Nancy and I lived on Lois Street in Aubrey, Sister Francis Carter and her family lived next door to us. I was backslidden and away from God at that time. But God had His plan in motion!

Sister Carter was indeed a woman of prayer. We knew that because back then, none of us had air conditioners, so we always had our windows open and up in the hot summertime. I could hear Sister Francis Carter praying and calling out my name in prayer, asking God to deal with me and not let me die and go to hell. Back then, it would make me kind of mad at times for her to pray like that! But I'm glad she did. And it was there on that very street where God got my attention. It was those prayers and others that positioned me to pray through and finally surrender to God's call to preach.

Now, fast forward to our time in Alba. Sister Carter, along with her daughter, came to hold a week-long children's crusade! During this Children's Crusade, several young people gave their hearts to God. One I know for sure was baptized with the Holy Ghost during the crusade. When the crusade was coming to an end, several of the adults came to me and asked if I could persuade Sister Carter to stay and preach for the Sunday morning service. She consented, and we had a beautiful service with the sweet presence of the Holy Spirit. Several young and old alike came to the altar. God was really moving in the Gunter Assembly of God.

It seemed to me that any time God begins to move and a church begins to grow, the devil starts to work overtime to bring it to a halt. I know God's Word tells us that He will not put more on us than we can bear but that He'll make a way of escape for us. But I was not finding any escape from the mounting stresses of life at that time. I began to stay physically exhausted in my body from working so many hours each day of the week. And then, within a short span of time, three drastic situations happened that profoundly affected me and my family. These events were like nothing we had experienced ever before in my lifetime.

One of these tragic events was that my older brother, Monroe, was found dead on his patio. The report said that he was sitting in a redwood lawn chair with his legs crossed and a bullet hole in his heart. The pistol was cocked again and was lying at least seven or more feet from where he was sitting. They said it was suicide, but in my mind, there were still a lot of unanswered questions. I don't feel at liberty to go into the other two situations at this time or in this book; perhaps at another time, I might feel free to talk or write about them.

Nevertheless, as a result of the perpetual tiredness and the incredible stress of those three life-altering events, in January 1982, I resigned as pastor of the Gunter Assembly of God in Alba, Texas. I never renewed my license to preach with the North Texas District of the Assemblies of God. I moved my family back to my hometown of Aubrey, Texas, and I grieved so profoundly over my brother's death that I nearly destroyed my relationship with all my family and close friends.

As hard as it might be to believe, I completely stopped going to church. (Thank God Nancy stayed in church with the kids and never gave up on serving God.) Once Shannon turned 16, he and his girlfriend Donna decided to quit school and get married. They promised to live with Nancy and me until they were eighteen, so we gave our consent.

Shannon and Donna lived with us for two years. Nathan was only one year old when they got married. Later, when Nathanael started school, he told his teacher that he had two sisters. His teacher knew us and knew Renee was our only daughter, but Nathan kept insisting that he had two sisters. Nancy finally figured out that he thought Donna was his sister, too.

My brother-in-law, Kenneth Wilson, furnished us with a piece of land and the money so that I could build us a story and a half house to live in. I think my brother-in-law really wanted to do this to help keep my mind from dwelling so much on my older brother's death.

Shannon came to work with me in the construction business and started helping with my construction jobs. Over time, I developed a reputable subcontracting business, and together, we did drywall, ceilings, doors, and framing for general contractors.

Unfortunately, although we had a good reputation for our quality work, I would often get into arguments and fights with others on the job. I lost a $200,000 door contract and was kicked out of a high-rise building for whipping the building manager.

I stayed in a backslidden condition for over three years. My heart became cold and hard. It was common for me to work for thirty-two hours without stopping. I didn't want to talk about church or God. I was angry at the world. Every now and then, I would get under conviction. I tried praying, but it seemed my prayers were in vain.

Finally, one Sunday night, while Nancy and the other family members were in church, I stayed home, sitting in my recliner, flipping through the TV channels. As I landed on one channel, Brother R. W. Schambach was on. Before I could change the channel, Brother Schambach pointed his big old finger at the camera and said, "Don't you turn that knob!" He said, "There's a backslid Pentecostal preacher watching me right now, and God said you've tried praying before, and He would not hear you. But God is saying now, tonight, if you get up out of that chair and kneel and pray, He will hear you." Me, I'm over there thinking, "Yeah, over a million people are watching, and there have got to be several backslid preachers watching." But then, all of a sudden, the thought popped into my mind, "What if it's me that he's talking to?"

I gradually slid out of the recliner and knelt to pray. God Almighty opened the windows of heaven and once again poured out His Spirit on and in me. I'll forever be thankful to God for more chances than one with His mercy and grace.

When Nancy and the kids came home from Sunday night church service, she walked into the room where I was sitting. I never said a word. She smiled, looked at me, and said, "You have prayed through!" I said, "How do you know?" She said, "I felt the sweet Spirit just as soon as we walked through the door."

Chapter Seven

Once you've been a pastor, it's hard to find a church and a pastor who will accept you into their church congregation. With my life back on track with God, I realized it would be a hard road to travel with my fellow man. "A lot of people won't have any confidence in a person after a dark time like I went through," I thought to myself, "I just can't pick up where I left off." No, I knew it would take some time to prove myself to the church world. But God had brought me out of that dark place, and I knew that He would take me through my next seasons, too.

I'm forever thankful that Nancy stayed with me through it all. She never gave up on me. That young girl that I was accused of robbing the cradle for was one strong, smart, loving woman.

Finally making steps forward and back in fellowship with the Lord, we began attending a Baptist church not far from where we lived. After Nancy and I had visited the church several times, the pastor asked us if we wanted to join the church. I questioned what that would consist of doing to be a member of the church. He said all that Nancy would have to do was transfer her membership letter from the Baptist church that she had joined when she was nine years old.

As for me, however, he said that I would have to come down front, make my confession of faith, and then be baptized by a Baptist minister before I could join the church. I'd already pastored four different churches, and I knew I was already saved and filled with baptism by the Holy Ghost! I looked at the pastor, smiled, and said, *"That'll never happen."*

Nancy and I visited several other churches within a reasonable driving distance. The Aubrey Assembly of God (that I grew up in) was still there, but it was full of a lot of my kin folks. Many of these kin folks never felt I was called to preach to start with. I had one cousin there who was of the opinion that anytime someone got too lazy to work, they always felt called to preach. And many church people, you know, they don't gossip. They *share.* (The only thing is that some of them share a little too much from time to time!) Anyway, during that season of life, Nancy and I never really felt welcome when we attended services there, so we moved on and kept looking.

I soon buried myself in my work. I worked long hours every day and often worked nights as well. I was skilled at building interior lease spaces and hanging office doors in high-rise buildings in the Dallas-Fort Worth area. I soon earned the title of "Door King" with several of the general contractors that I subcontracted from.

When the JCPenney Company moved their headquarters from up north down to Dallas, Texas, they leased thirty-nine temporary floors at the Lincoln Towers. When they started contracting out the demolition and reconstruction of those thirty-nine floors, I subcontracted eleven of the floors. I put together a seventeen-man crew, including me. We had completed seven of the eleven floors already when I was diagnosed with cancer.

The doctors had discovered a tumor the size of a tennis ball connected to my right kidney. The tumor was attached to the main blood vessel that feeds the lower part of my body. On the 5th of June 1989, they operated on me and removed the tumor and my right kidney. The doctor said the cancer peeled off from the main blood vessel that it was attached to, just like peeling a banana. Well, *there was a reason for that!*

Before surgery, the doctor expressed concern that the blood vessel would burst during surgery and I would bleed to death. But before they carried me into the operating room, four elderly ladies from my home church came into my hospital room to anoint me with oil and to pray for me. Through their prayers that morning, God placed His healing hand on my body and guided the surgeon's hands that day. And I'm still here, cancer-free to this day.

I was off work eleven months after my surgery. Since I had only finished seven of the eleven floors for the contracted JCPenney renovation prior to my surgery, my oldest son, Shannon, stepped up to supervise the finishing of the last four floors at Lincoln Center. He was indeed a God-send in finishing the contracted jobs.

During the time that I couldn't work, things got very slim at our house. My sweet Nancy went to work in the cash office at one of the local Walmart stores to help keep us afloat during this time. Soon after, she started working at the Wisdom Center, a ministry in a nearby town.

While Nancy was working at Walmart, she got paid $300.00 every two weeks. My medicine alone cost over $600 a month, and we had no insurance. A Baptist friend of ours started paying for my medicine each month, and that was a big help!

Whatever the request, Nancy always gave it her best. Later, she opened a cafe called "Grandma Nancy's." Nancy loved to cook, and I loved her and her cooking. Nancy served breakfast, dinner, and supper every day when the cafe was open. She ran the restaurant for about a year and a half until her hips and knees started hurting her so bad that she sold the cafe.

I can't say that we were never without, but we were never without for long. God saw us through it all. Yes, he'll make a way where there seems to be no way. The

Methodist church brought groceries two different times to our front door.

At the time of my diagnosis, our three oldest children were grown and married, but our fourth child, Nathanael (Nathan), was only nine years old, so of course, he still lived at home. When Nancy took him to school, he begged her to let him out a block from the school because he was ashamed of our old car. We lost our good car because we couldn't make the payments, but we were able to buy a much older car for Nancy to drive back and forth to work. The car's headliner was falling apart so badly, but Nancy pinned it up to make do. The car's paint was faded, and it just generally looked terrible.

That year, for Christmas, Nathan had printed out a Christmas list of things he hoped to receive. We knew it was impossible for us to provide these items that year, but Nancy had prayed over it, and we shared this list with only Jesus. The next thing we knew, one of my first cousins had it on their heart to purchase gifts for our youngest son's Christmas that year—everything that was on his little list was under the Christmas tree! Yes, God is God in the good times, and he's still God in the not-so-good times.

Once I recovered, some of my friends talked me into running for City Council in our hometown. I ran and won the seat that I had signed up for. After being seated on the council, they voted me in as Mayor Pro Tem. This was in May of 1994. In July of 1994, the mayor resigned, and I then became Mayor of Aubrey until May 1999.

While I was mayor of Aubrey, I received a phone call from Pastor Harold Bowman of Aubrey First Baptist Church. He knew I was a Pentecostal preacher and that I was also a carpenter. (And, evidently, Pastor Bowman also knew about the reason I didn't join the other Baptist church.) It turns out that First Baptist was right in the middle of a building program at the time, and some type of disagreement caused a split. Several of the deacons and people had left the church. Pastor Bowman asked me if I would consider coming to help him finish the trim work in the educational part of the building. He also asked if I would be interested in joining the church and helping pull it back together again. He told me that he would accept my confession of faith and my baptismal certificate if I wanted to join First Baptist Church.

Nancy and I did join First Baptist Church, and later, they ordained me as a Baptist minister. I taught a Sunday school class and often preached, even though they all knew that I was Pentecostal. Nancy and I attended and worked with Pastor Bowman for over four years before we felt led to start a new independent church in Krugerville, Texas.

We began the independent church plant in Krugerville in a space I found for lease at one end of a metal office building. I framed space for an office, a Sunday school room, and a kitchen in the 1800 square feet of space. Drywall Interiors of Dallas kindly donated the drywall and metal framing for the walls. I used some old carpet samples for the floor.

We named the new church Grace Temple. In the beginning, attendance was in the low teens but soon grew into the twenties. Sometimes, we'd be in the thirties for attendance. We had several saved; at least two that I remembered were filled with the Holy Ghost, and I baptized eight people one Sunday afternoon in a friend's swimming pool. (One strong man that I baptized that day was afraid of water. I like to have never got him all the way under the water! It was a wrestling match for quite a while before I won and finally soused him under.) We enjoyed our fellowship at Grace Temple, where we pastored for seven years and four months before I felt the release of the burden to continue. At that time, we encouraged the people to find another local church and stay faithful in serving the Lord.

Some weeks later, Nancy and I stopped at the Pilot Point Dairy Queen for a snack. Brother Steve Newman and his wife, Sister Louetta Newman, were already there and asked us to come and sit with them. They shared that the Denton Section of the Assemblies of God had asked them if they would pray about reopening the Tioga Assembly of God. The church had been closed for a year or more. The Newmans asked Nancy and me if we would consider coming and helping them if they decided to take on the reopening of the Tioga church. We told them we would. This was in 2011 when we started attending Tioga Assembly of God with Pastors Steve and Louetta Newman. Nancy and I moved to Mountain Springs, about six miles from Tioga. (The country singer Randy Travis lived just 7/10 of a mile down the road from us.) We taught Sunday school and preached quite a bit for Brother Newman at the Tioga church. Nancy and I felt welcome and we didn't feel any friction whatsoever while working with the Newmans at the Tioga church. We worked with them for a little over five years before we moved on.

One Saturday morning, Sister Joyce Evans, a lifelong friend, called and asked me if I would bring Nancy to a rental property of hers in Krugerville. She had a renter moving out, and she needed to inspect the house to see whether to give the renter her deposit back. Nancy and I drove down to Krugerville and brought with us two folding chairs so the ladies could sit and visit while her son and I inspected the house. As I walked into the front room where Nancy and Sister Evans were sitting, Sister Evans spoke up and said, "Gene Paul King, God told me to tell you that you need to go pastor the church in Throckmorton, Texas." I laughed and asked her if God had told her anything else I needed to know. At that time, I didn't even know where Throckmorton, Texas, was! But what she said stayed with me the rest of the day.

When Nancy and I got back home that afternoon, I got a map of Texas out and located Throckmorton. That same afternoon, Nancy and I drove over to Throckmorton and found the little church and parsonage. She and I walked around the building and prayed for God's will to be done. The next day, I called the Abilene Sectional

Presbyter, and he scheduled me to preach at the New Life Assembly of God in Throckmorton the following Sunday.

Nancy and I took a vote of confidence from the people, and it was 100 percent. The presbyter and sectional committee appointed Nancy and me as pastors of the Throckmorton church. This was in the early part of 2016, and only seven people were attending the New Life Assembly of God in Throckmorton.

God began to bless the church, and soon, other people started attending our church services. People with a lot of hurt in their personal lives seemed drawn to our congregation. Three couples that were just living together got married without me saying a word about it. One family came that had lost a child to suicide. Another family came that had lost a child in a truck accident. Another lady had divorced her husband after discovering that he had molested her sisters when they were young.

Two families were experiencing wounded relationships because the children and grandchildren were being rejected because of what some termed "interracial marriages" within the family. So, there were a lot of hurting hearts coming to find recovery and restoration. Through it all, God was moving and putting the broken vessels back together again.

We baptized nine people one Sunday afternoon in Lake Throckmorton. God blessed the church financially, too. We soon had over twenty voting members and requested that the Section set the church in order so that it could operate independently without sectional guidance. Within a year and a half, we were averaging forty-five in attendance on Sunday mornings. One Easter, we had eighty-eight, and our little church was packed.

There are only three cities in Throckmorton County: Throckmorton (the county seat), which had a population of 700-plus; Woodson, with 300-plus; and Elbert, which had another thirty or so. The remaining folks lived out in the country on cattle ranches and farms. But the whole county had less than 1200 people. So our little church that grew from seven to averaging forty-five on Sundays, I'd say, was hitting a pretty good average.

On the last Sunday of each month, the church would have a luncheon after the morning service. The church annex was a house that was next door to the church. At these meals, my sweet Nancy would always fix my plate and bring it to me. I never made her do it. She did it because she wanted to do it. But most of the older women of the church would tell me the "what for" because Nancy always fixed my plate and brought it to me. I'd say to them, "Leave it alone! It took me years to train her to do it for me!" Of course, I was kidding (kind of). One Sunday, a young couple saw Nancy bring my plate to me. And the young man asked me how I got her to do that for me. Before I could answer, his wife said, "Don't even think about it!"

As the church grew in number, parking soon became a problem. We had a vacant lot between the church and the annex house. Thankfully, we had a heavy equipment operator who attended our church and worked on one of the local ranches. He brought the ranch's road grader and bladed the vacant lot for us. Five different people donated five belly dump loads of crushed rock for the new parking lot.

Yes, God blessed the church and its people in various ways. But with blessings always come sad times as life goes forward. Sad events began to happen one after another. We lost five men from the church over five years. The first one died, I'd say, of a natural death in his early nineties. The second one passed away, sitting in his recliner. The third man was killed in an automobile accident, the fourth died from a self-inflicted gunshot wound, and the fifth man died of heart failure after having stent surgery.

In 2020, the global pandemic hit, and the United States government shut the churches down. I followed their request for four Sundays in a row, and then I opened the church back up again. Just a few people came back to church; several were afraid that the government would have them fined or arrested. I really don't know why the others stayed away, but after a while, I learned that some were meeting and having church in different homes.

During the four Sundays the church was closed, several of the people wanted me to make videos and post them on Facebook. What I know about computers is so tiny that a penny matchbox would hold it and still have room for the matches. But one night, after Nancy had gone to bed, I was scrolling through my Facebook news-feed. The thought occurred to me to make a live broadcast of a ten-minute sermonette. By that time of night, I had already stripped down to my underwear at the time, so I thought, all I have to do is put my shirt back on. I thought I would just sit at my desk and the people would not know that I was only in my underwear from the waist down. (I know, *wrong decision*. You can see the disaster coming already, can't you?)

Well, I made the video just fine. I thought I had ended it, and it cut off the camera. Wrong. The camera was still running! Dummy me! I got up and began to parade around (move about) the room in my underwear. Suddenly, the house landline phone began to ring. Then my cell phone began to ring, and Nancy's cell phone also rang. Nancy got out of bed, yelling for me to cut that camera off!

I soon realized that I had more followers on my Facebook page than I thought! A Baptist preacher and his wife in Oklahoma were watching, and they had called. Our daughter called on her mother's cell phone to ask, "Is something wrong with Daddy? He is showing off his underwear on social media!"

Several of our church members were also watching. One lady called to ask if I was advertising for Hanes underwear, and another called to ask if I was advertising for Fruit of the Loom. I take it they got a good look. Thus, I ended my sermonette videos for a while. My sweet Nancy saw to that. (I still use social media for ministering, but never again without being fully clothed!)

Nancy and I prayed and asked God to see if it was time for us to move on. After a few weeks, we felt the burden lift and felt released to leave the church. Before we had a chance to officially resign, two of the deacons came and asked us to leave. I answered that Nancy and I had already decided we were resigning and going, but certainly not because they had asked us to leave.

I notified the Abilene Section Presbyter that Nancy and I would be leaving the church in Throckmorton. He immediately arranged to meet with the church people and the church board. The day after the Presbyter held the meeting, I received the following message from him:

Hello friend.

What I found out Thursday night was what I already suspected. The folks at the church need to repent. They had nothing of any consequence on you. All their complaints were silly little things that do not amount to much. Don't worry. I set the record straight!

I first taught from the Word of God about church unity and church government, and I explained that deacons do not have authority over the pastor. What they did was wrong and against their own bylaws. I informed them that, as a result, the church is now under District supervision, the board is dissolved, and all its members are dismissed.

I also told them they needed to repent for what they had done. Afterward, I entertained questions for a few minutes but shut it down as soon as I could see that all they wanted to do was complain. And all their complaints were just silly. I told them all to go home.

We have a lot of cleaning up to do because people have just let the devil control them. You don't need to feel bad. No pastor is perfect; we all make mistakes. But mistakes and dismissible offenses are two different things. I made it clear to them that you were not guilty of being fired.

Brother King, I have been through this very thing myself. I was fired from a church because the board got mad at me for how I preached and because they did not like my pastoral style. It's a terrible sin for a church to do this to a pastor. I know it hurts, but don't let it beat you down. You're a good man, and God has used you. He will still use you and can open new doors of ministry.

We love y'all and are praying for you.

The Abilene section paid Nancy and me severance pay and paid our moving expenses from the New Life Church's funds. We stored all our belongings in rental storage bins in Tioga, Texas. We moved in with our daughter, who lived in Denton. Nancy and I started attending Faith Tabernacle Assembly of God in Denton.

One afternoon, I received a text message from Brother Jack Stone, a friend of ours who has held several singing engagements with us in the past. He texted and said I needed to pray about putting my name in for the First Assembly of God in Childress, Texas. I told him we would pray about it and thanked him for letting us know about the church being open.

One night at Faith Tabernacle, Brother Terry Johnson was shaking hands with Nancy and me. Suddenly, just out of the clear blue sky. He said, "Brother King, I was driving through Childress and passed the church there. God impressed me to tell you to send them a resume." So here were two men of God telling Nancy and me to pray about contacting the First Assembly of God in Childress, Texas.

I called the church number, and the pastor, who was leaving the church, answered the phone. I visited with him on the phone for some time, and then I told him the church probably would not be interested in me because I was at the time 79 years old. The outgoing pastor laughed at me. I asked him what was so funny about that. And he said, "You're still young. I'm 87 years old, and they've put up with me."

I left our phone number with the former pastor, and he said he'd pass it on to one of the deacons. A day or two later, one of the deacons called and asked if Nancy and I could come up and fill in for the following weekend services. I told him we could and would be there, the Good Lord willing.

At Faith Tabernacle's midweek service in Denton, I was telling Brother Terry Johnson that the Childress church had called and asked us to come in and fill in for them the following Sunday. Brother Johnson laughed and said, "It's a tryout, and they'll vote on you." I answered, "No, Brother Johnson, I'm just filling in for the weekend services." Once again, he laughed and said, "No, Brother King, they'll vote on you, and you will be their new pastor."

We drove over to Childress that Saturday afternoon and spent the night in the church's annex. We preached Sunday morning, and right after I got through preaching, the deacon in charge asked if it would be alright if they voted on us. I thought, why not? They asked Nancy and me to step out into the church entrance while they voted. In a little bit, they called us back to the auditorium. Guess what? It happened just like Brother Terry Johnson said it would. (I've often wondered why God would tell him what would happen and not tell me. But far be it from me to tell God what to do!) The vote was 100 percent, and they extended the invitation to us to pastor the First Assembly of God in Childress, Texas.

FIRST ASSEMBLY OF GOD, CHILDRESS, TX
(THE LAST CHURCH THAT GENE AND NANCY PASTORED TOGETHER
BEFORE MOVING BACK TO AUBREY, TX IN JANUARY, 2023.)

Chapter Eight

Nancy and I came to the First Assembly of God, Childress, Texas, in the latter part of 2021. The church wanted to have the inside of the parsonage painted before we moved in, so Nancy and I drove back and forth from Denton to Childress for several weekends until the parsonage was ready for us to move in.

In the previous stories, I chronicled the ages of each member of the immediate family when we made the move to each new hometown. With this move, however, all of our children were grown and it was just Nancy and me moving into the parsonage in Childress. Still, our kids didn't miss out! Our children rented two U-Haul trucks to move us. Shannon, Donna, Bubba, and Renee helped load and unload our belongings. When they were hooking up our washer and dryer, they noticed that we were using a pair of vice grips in place of the knob on our dryer. One of them told Anthony, who lives in North Carolina, about the condition of the dryer and the vice grips. Anthony called and told his mom that a new washer and dryer would be delivered to us the very next day. *God truly blessed us with children who honor their parents.*

After we had settled in, we started having church on Sunday mornings, plus we added a service on Sunday nights and a Bible study on Wednesday nights. Before we arrived, they only had church on Sunday mornings.

After a few weeks, we invited several Assemblies of God pastors from other cities to come for a Saturday morning service. Afterward, we had a time of fellowship at lunch, which was served in our church annex. Five pastors came that Saturday: Brother Jason Houston, the former pastor at First Assembly of God, Clarendon, Texas (now in Kansas City, Missouri); Brother Dale Griswold, the pastor at First Assembly of God, Memphis, Texas; Sister Geraldine Savage, the pastor at First Assembly of God, Paducah, Texas; Brother Kenton Johnson, the pastor at First Assembly of God, Shamrock, Texas; and Brother Jeremy Walters, the pastor at First Assembly of God, Quanah, Texas.

After lunch that Saturday, all the pastors held a meeting. They voted to start having a fellowship meeting once a month and rotate the location from church to church. We all agreed to rotate preaching at the services as well. It was decided to call the gatherings "Circle Fellowship

Meetings." A few months later, Brother Joe Bushnell, the pastor at Holliday Assembly of God, Holliday, Texas, also joined our Circle Fellowship group. The Holy Spirit showed up and blessed everyone at the Circle Fellowship meetings each month.

As we learned a bit about the history of the Childress church, we found out that the church would be one hundred years old the year after we arrived. The existing building was not that old because the first building was at a different location in another part of town, but the church itself was coming up on its 100-year anniversary in 2022.

The church began to make plans for a Centennial celebration. The church sent invitations to all former pastors we could locate. We also sent invitations to many former members of the church, inviting them to come and celebrate the church's 100th birthday with us. West Texas District Superintendent Brother Glen R. Beaver brought forth the message at the celebration. Sectional Presbyter Brother Raymond Mizelle ministered over our communion service. Three former pastors were able to attend: Brother Gary McClendon, Brother Neil Urwin, and Brother LR Halston. Each of them blessed us in Word and song. It was an outstanding service that Sunday morning, and everyone had a great time visiting and having lunch with old and new friends.

Toward the end of 2022, sweet Nancy's mind began to fail her. The doctor diagnosed her with the first stage of dementia. She had diabetes, and when her blood sugar dropped, she would become confused and wouldn't know where she was or what she was doing. She wanted to go back to our hometown, Aubrey, Texas, every week. Our son Nathan and his family had a home in Aubrey. Our daughter Renee lived in Denton, which is only 12 miles from Aubrey. But it was almost a three-and-a-half-hour drive one way from Childress to the Denton/Aubrey area.

We began to pray for God to heal her or give us the wisdom to make the right decisions as to what she and I should do concerning our future and if we should stay as pastors of the church. Although I knew that Nancy's mind might become worse day by day, leaving the pastorate would eliminate any extra income. With just the income from our Social Security checks, we couldn't afford to pay rent and live in the Aubrey area.

One morning my younger brother Gaylon called, and Nancy answered the phone. My brother told her he knew of a house that we could rent that would be affordable with our income. From that moment on, there was no way I could ever change her mind about moving back to our hometown. I met with the church deacon board and told them we would be resigning and leaving the church.

In the latter part of January 2023, our wonderful children once again paid for the move, loaded us up, and moved us back to our hometown of Aubrey. On June 14th of that year, Nancy and I celebrated 60 years of marriage. Four days later, on June 19th, Nancy started hurting in her stomach and her back. I took her to the Emergency

Room at Medical City Hospital in Denton. They scanned her and discovered that she had cancer in her liver and her lungs, a mass in her stomach, and also a mass in her lower back. The doctor said it was already Stage 4 cancer. We had no idea! She and I both thought our aches and pains were just from growing old.

The doctors said she was too far along to give her chemotherapy or radiation treatments. We began to pray for God to heal her or perform a miracle on her. The doctor sent us to Dallas for a PET scan, which showed cancer cells in nearly every organ inside her body. They gave her medicine for her pain and sent her home.

About one month later, on July 18, Nancy got to hurting so bad that I carried her back to the Emergency Room in Denton. They admitted her to the 4th floor of the hospital, where she remained for four days. The primary doctor told her we needed to take her home and get set up with Hospice care. However, before we left, the Oncologist (Nancy's cancer doctor) stepped in and told me that she wouldn't live long enough for us to get set up with Hospice at home. The doctor had found an available room in the intensive care unit on the third floor of the hospital. The doctor assured us that they could move her there and the nurses would take very good care of her in the final moments.

The doctor was correct. The ICU nurses were wonderful in their care of my sweet Nancy in her final moments. Just two days after moving her into the intensive care unit on the third floor of the hospital, at around 2:00 a.m. on the morning of July 24, 2023, Nancy Ruth Cranmore King left all of us to be with Jesus.

I want to conclude this final chapter (and Nancy's final chapter here on earth) with a conversation I had with my sweet Nancy during that last week on the fourth floor of the hospital.

One night, around midnight, Nancy called me over to her bedside. She smiled and asked me if I remembered some of the conversations that she and I would have when we were a young married couple lying in bed. I answered, "The ones about heaven?" And she smiled and said, "Yes."

My thoughts raced back through the years to our early days when she would ask me things like, "Will we be married once we are in heaven?" I would answer, "Baby, I don't know." And she would reply, "If you're going to preach, you'd better find out."

I said, "Paul said we would be known as we were known, but Jesus said that in the resurrection, they neither marry nor are given in marriage." She would reply, "But we're already married." I told her she had a good point there!

Sometimes, she would ask me, "Will we live in the same mansion? Or would I have one, and you have one?" And again, I'd say, "Baby, I don't know." And she would say that if I was going to preach, I had better find out!

That night in the hospital in July of 2023, both of us remembering those conversations early in life, she smiled and took my hand and said, "Daddy, unless God gives me a miracle, I'm going to find out all the answers to all those questions before you do."

With tears in my eyes, I tried to smile back at her. I told her, "Yes, it looks that way. And you have always loved to beat me in anything we ever done. And I know I would sometimes act like I was mad about that. But deep down inside, I loved to see the sparkle in your eyes when you would win at whatever it was."

My sweet Nancy beat me one final time,
completing her race ahead of mine.

Epilogue

She is far more precious than jewels, and her value is far above that of rubies or pearls. The heart of her husband trusts in her confidently and relies on and believes in her securely...

She comforts, encourages, and does him only good as long as there is life within her. Her husband is known in the gates, when he sits among the elders of the land.

Strength and dignity are her clothing and her position is strong and secure;

she rejoices over the future ... knowing that she and her family are in readiness for it!

Her children rise up and call her blessed and her husband boasts of and praises her, saying,

Many daughters have done virtuously, nobly, and well, but (in our lives) she excelled them all...[35]

Because... she loved.

Thankful for Us

(Selected photos from the stories within this book.)

"My Nancy, sweet and fancy...
In any crowd,
she always made me proud!"

Gene King

60TH WEDDING ANNIVERSARY
JUNE 14, 2023

NANCY JULY 2023
(LAST PHOTO)

147

Appendix

Notes

1   William Iley King (1909-1985)

2   Abbie Katherine (Wilson) King (1914-2013)

3   Leon Odell Brockett (1918-1996), son of Haley Young Brockett and Eliza (Elizabeth) Josephine (Close) Brockett, and married Dorothy L. (Wilson) Brockett in 1939.

4   William Monroe King (1935-1981)

5   Jimmy Carroll King (1938-2023)

6   Lois Kathryn (King) Harmon (1932-2018)

7   Edward Franklin Cranmore (1918-1978)

8   May Marie (Sons) Cranmore (1925-1989)

9   Carolyn Sue (Cranmore) Wilson (1945-2020)

10   City Cafe, downtown Aubrey, Texas

11   Kenneth Wayne Wilson (1944-)

12   Rev. Raymond Y. Grimes (1931-2016) was a minister for over 60 years for the Assemblies Of God. ("Raymond Grimes Obituary (1931 - 2016) - Fort Worth, TX - Star-Telegram," Legacy.com, June 23, 2016, https://www.legacy.com/us/obituaries/dfw/name/raymond-grimes-obituary?id=11815300.)

13   Dr. Gerald Patrick Flanagan was born May 12, 1921 in Ft. Worth to parents A. J. and Yvette Flanagan. In the early 1960's he became Co-owner of the Denton Osteopathic Hospital. During his tenure at the hospital, he along with Dr. Art Wiley, became the first D.O.'s to have privileges at the County (Flow) Memorial Hospital (where Renee King would be born two years later). ("Gerald Flanagan Obituary (2012) - Argyle, TX - Dallas Morning News," Legacy.com, May 1, 2012, https://obits.dallasnews.com/us/obituaries/dallasmorningnews/name/gerald-flanagan-obituary?id=21371034.]

14   The "old Flow Hospital" (where both Renee and Nathan were born) was The James Flow Memorial Hospital which opened in 1950. It was a nonprofit city-county hospital that played an important role in Denton for thirty-eight years. The hospital was demolished in 2002 to make way for a single-room occupancy student housing complex. (Annetta Ramsay, "Flow Hospital Played

Important Role in Denton for 38 Years," Denton Record-Chronicle, June 6, 2021, https://dentonrc.com/news/flow-hospital-played-important-role-in-denton-for-38-years/article_94dcadb8-258f-543f-98b1-e50f2d-c3f6eb.html.)

15   Shannon Gene King (1965-)

16   Anthony Paul King (1967-)

17   Regena Renee King (1969-)

18   Nathanael Paul King(1980-)

19   LZ Harmon, Sr. (1926-2022) was born August 13, 1926, in Aubrey, Texas, to Jacob Arthur & Talley (Brockett) Harmon. LZ married Lois Kathryn King on February 11, 1947, in Aubrey, Texas. He was a general contractor and real estate developer in the North Texas area. He was a deacon and worship leader at Assembly of God in Aubrey, Texas. As a public servant, he served multiple terms on the Aubrey School Board, Aubrey City Council and proudly served as the mayor of Aubrey. ("LZ Harmon Sr. Obituary, October 2022", Slay Memorial Funeral Home, 2022, https://www.slaymemorialfuneralhome.com/obituaries/Lz-Harmon/#!/Obituary.

20   Otto David Wilson (1914-1998) was born on June 14, 1914 to Elisha Elias Wilson (1869-1942) and Nannie (Bradley) Wilson (1873-1923) in Collin County, Texas, and married Wilma Inez Wilson in 1939. (FindAGrave. com, accessed July 7, 2024, https://www.findagrave.com/memorial/13436391/otto-david-wilson

21   Samuel Patterson "Pat" Burchett (1881-1978) was born in Virginia to William M. and Martha (unknown maiden name) Burchett. He moved to Pilot Point area in Texas as a farm hand and later married Harriet Emily (Ford) Burchett (1887-1937), of Tennessee, daughter of Henry Gutton Ford and Rosinah (Bishop) Ford of Scott, Virginia. (Find A Grave, accessed July 7, 2024, https://www.findagrave.com/memorial/62399671/samuel-patterson-burchett.) (Wikitree.com, accessed July 7, 2024, https://www.wikitree.com/wiki/Ford-10685)

22   Wilma Inez Wilson (1916-2010), 94 of Aubrey, passed away Friday, December 03, 2010 in Corinth. She was born on July 14, 1916 in Denton County to Fred and Velma (Starr) Daniel. She married Otto D. Wilson; Wilma Wilson Obituary, 2010, https://www.heartlandfuneralhome.net/obituaries/Wilma-Wilson-23013/#!/Obituary.

23   LH Kruger (1924-2021) was born May 24, 1924 in Aubrey, TX to Henry and Lela (Sauls) Krueger. LH

married Willie Mae Wilson on November 10, 1945 in Decatur, TX. She preceded him in death on February 17, 2015. LH later married Doris Marie Patterson in Aubrey, TX on August 25, 2017. LH served in the United States Army during World War II. In 1964, LH Kruger purchased 328 acres of land off of Highway 377 just south of Aubrey, TX, which became the community of Krugerville. In 1973 the city of Krugerville was incorporated. At some point, the spelling of the last name changed from Krueger to Kruger in modern generations. ("LH Kruger Obituary," accessed July 7, 2024, https://www.slaymemorialfuneralhome.com/obituaries/Lh-Kruger/#!/Obituary.)

24   Charlotte Loreta Grimes (1931-2022), 90, passed away Tuesday, Feb. 8, 2022. She was born Dec. 9, 1931, in Greenville, Texas to Raymond and Edna Gibson. Charlotte married Rev. Raymond Y. Grimes, Sr. in 1948. She was preceded in death by her husband Raymond in 2016; and her parents. ("Obituary for Charlotte Loreta Grimes," Greenwood Funeral Home, 2022, accessed on July 7, 2024, https://www.greenwoodfuneralhomes.com/obituary/charlotte-grimes.)

25   Carl and Ola McFatridge moved to Whitewright in August 1955 and leased a former food locker plant. Operation has an inauspicious start the following September 25, 1955 when just one hog was butchered. It was some time before more than a half dozen hogs were

butchered in a full day. Ola McFatridge (whose husband died five years later) ground the meat, mixed and stuffed the sausage, and delivered the bags to seven Whitewright stores. The company's colorful history that had a one-pig start but reached a dramatic climax in 1966 when Carl's Tasty Sausage received the prestigious gold medal awarded by the International Institute for Quality Selection, with headquarters at Brussels, Belgium. More than that, the triumph was repeated in 1987 and 1988, with palms added to the seal the latter year for extra merit in competition with foods from throughout the world. The gold symbol appears on every roll of Carl's Sausage. The competitions were held in Brussels, Geneva and Athens. Ola McFatridge died June 20, 2008, at the age of 100 years and nine months; her death month and day were the same as her husband's in 1960. She was born in Celina, Collin Co., Texas on September 27, 1907, the daughter of Albert & Katy Kerr. (Grayson County TX GenWeb, accessed Jul 8, 2024, https://usgenwebsites.org/TXGrayson/ANewLand/Towns/Whitewright/CarlsSausage/CarlsSausage.html.)

26   Summit View Church, "Our Story," Howe, Texas, accessed July 7, 2024, https://www.summitviewhowe.com/our-story.

27   Evangelist J. R. Kneggs was nicknamed "Shoutin' Kneggs," and he was an Assemblies of God minister.

Brother J. R. Kneggs was married to Ruby (Jones) Kneggs for 50 years. They made their home in Greenville. They enjoyed their years together in ministry to people from all walks of life. He was born on January 19, 1912 in Bonham, Texas, and preceded Sister Ruby in death on February 27, 1983 in Greenville, Hunt County, Texas. Sister Ruby was born on January 15, 1915, in Telephone, Texas, to Ernest and Hettie Jones; she passed away in Mesquite, TX, on November 6, 2011, at the age of 96.

28   Sgt Clint Haggard Krantz, was a US Army World War II veteran. He was born October 25, 1922 and passed away on June 10, 1998, in Sherman, Texas. An interesting connecting fact is that Brother Krantz was married to Bertie Jewel (Burchett) Krantz (1931-2000), the granddaughter of Elder Pat Burchett, one of the senior men who many years before came to church after work every night to pray with me in my younger years. (See Page 42 and Endnote 19). Sister Krantz was born in 1931 to Hervie Milen Burchett and Fannie Ethel (Mullins) Burchett, Elder Burchett's son and daughter-in-law.

29   The Russell-Newman Manufacturing Company's philosophy was 'What was good for the community was good for the company.' From humble beginnings to revolutionizing the lingerie industry, the manufacturer was a strong fixture in Denton County for over 70 years. The company was founded on June 1, 1939, and the products

included women's lingerie and sleepwear for women and children. *In 1953, Russell-Newman opened a factory in Pilot Point,* where they began catching national attention, designing products that caught the interest of companies like Playtex and JC Penney. [Citation and credit for the photo below: Denton County History and Culture, "A Historic Denton County Business: Russell-Newman," June 22, 2018, accessed July 8, 2024, https://dentoncountyhistoryandculture.wordpress.com/2018/06/22/a-historic-denton-county-business-russell-newman/

PILOT POINT SEWING FACTORY - RUSSELL-NEWMAN

30   "Our Story," SummitViewHowe.com

31   "Our Story," SummitViewHowe.com

32   As of 2024, the beautiful pastures of Sugar Hill Farms (where the author and his family often rode horses) still exist in Arkansas and recently sold with approximately 932 acres of highly improved registered cattle land.

SUGAR HILL FARMS, NEAR OZARK, ARKANSAS

33   Lyrics.com, STANDS4 LLC, 2024. "The Strawberry Roan Lyrics." Accessed July 8, 2024. https://www.lyrics.com/lyric/18908738/Marty+Robbins/The+Strawberry+Roan.

34   Skaggs, Ricky, "Honey (Open the Door)", February 1984, (Lyrics: Mel Tillis, 1962)

35   Proverbs 31:10-12,23,25,28-29 adapted from AMPC

36   Roseville Assembly Of God Ozark Arkansas , Roseville Assembly Of God Ozark Arkansas Facebook Page Image, accessed August 9, 2024, https://www.facebook.com/profile.php?id=100071712856620&sk=about.

About the Author

In July 2023, Brother Gene King's world turned upside down. After sixty years of marriage, he had to say goodbye to the love of his life, the queen of his heart, his sweet Nancy.

In his own words, Brother King says, "Having to learn to live without her by my side has been the most trying thing I have ever had to experience in my entire life. But with God's help I'm still going forward with my life. The encouragement of my children and grandchildren to write this book has helped me remember both happy and sad times that Nancy and I lived through together and the many times God heard and answered our prayers."

Brother King has already begun writing his next book about growing up in a small town (a prequel to this memoir). When not writing or preaching, he enjoys having breakfast at a local cafe with old friends and meeting new ones. He enjoys listening to country gospel music and using social media as a ministry tool.

Brother King still preaches from time to time in the local church where he now attends. He is also available to minister elsewhere at weekend or midweek services.

To invite Brother Gene King to preach
or to purchase additional copies of this book,
please contact him by mail:
Brother Gene Paul King
PO Box 416
Aubrey, Texas 76227

(Additional copies may also be purchased
at all major online retail book sellers.)

www.ingramcontent.com/pod-product-compliance
Lightning Source LLC
Chambersburg PA
CBHW051200120626
46547CB00012B/1134